Using Artificial Intelligence in Term Papers and Theses

Fabian Lang

Using Artificial Intelligence in Term Papers and Theses

A Practical Guide for Students with Actionable Recommendations, Prompt Examples, and Critical Reflections

Springer

Fabian Lang
Faculty of Business & Computer Science
Hannover University of Applied Sciences
and Arts
Hannover, Niedersachsen, Germany

ISBN 978-3-662-73207-6 ISBN 978-3-662-73208-3 (eBook)
https://doi.org/10.1007/978-3-662-73208-3

Translation from the German language edition: "Künstliche Intelligenz in Seminar- und Abschlussarbeiten" by Fabian Lang, © Der/die Herausgeber bzw. der/die Autor(en), exklusiv lizenziert an Springer-Verlag GmbH, DE, ein Teil von Springer Nature 2025. Published by Springer Berlin Heidelberg. All Rights Reserved.

This book is a translation of the original German edition "Künstliche Intelligenz in Seminar- und Abschlussarbeiten" by Fabian Lang, published by Springer-Verlag GmbH, DE in 2025. The translation was done with the help of an artificial intelligence machine translation tool. A subsequent human revision was done primarily in terms of content, so that the book will read stylistically differently from a conventional translation. Springer Nature works continuously to further the development of tools for the production of books and on the related technologies to support the authors.

This Springer imprint is published by the registered company Springer-Verlag GmbH, DE, part of Springer Nature.
The registered company address is: Heidelberger Platz 3, 14197 Berlin, Germany

Preface

Until the mid-19th century, whale oil was primarily used to fuel lamps. When petroleum emerged in the 1860s as an oil-based alternative to the core product of whaling, the profession of whaler in Europe disappeared almost entirely within a few years. This history demonstrates that technological progress can trigger short-term uncertainty and profound change, even if long-term benefits arise. Similarly disruptive changes are expected from artificial intelligence (AI). Unlike whaling, which affected only a single profession, AI will impact nearly all knowledge-based occupations. While few traditional professions will disappear entirely, job profiles will fundamentally change. AI will become an integral part of knowledge work and, as a key competency, will have a lasting impact on professional practice.

This transformation does not stop at universities, which are also facing profound changes. Academic education—shaped by centuries of tradition—must now adapt to a new, digital reality. The first years following the launch of ChatGPT, in particular, were marked by uncertainty for both instructors and students. Many were concerned about attempts at deception and the loss of academic values. I myself was initially skeptical, especially due to the limited capabilities of early AI systems. However, with growing experience and the rapid technological advancements, I, like the vast majority of my colleagues, have become convinced that AI is here to stay, and that this technology will permanently accompany us in both academic work and education.

This transformation is often difficult for students to interpret as well. On the one hand, they want to act responsibly and avoid the risk of accidental deception; on the other hand, there is often a lack of clear, consistent guidance on how to handle AI. This leads to uncertainty, but also to significant differences in usage: some students use AI in a very targeted way, while others avoid it out of concern for mistakes or sanctions. This behavior further widens the gap in competencies: those who are already strong students become even better through AI, while others—due to lack of time or doubts—hardly benefit from its possibilities.

This Matthew effect[1] was one of the main reasons for writing this book. The goal is to bring as many students as possible to a common and secure level in

[1]Matthew 25:29 (RSV): "For to every one who has will more be given, and he will have abundance; but from him who has not, even what he has will be taken away."

dealing with AI. Initial positive experiences from my courses on research methods have shown me how great the need and interest are.

The second motivation was to prepare the topic on a scientifically sound basis and to create a textbook that goes beyond the predominantly grey literature available so far. While there are numerous guidelines, blog posts, and social media posts, scientific contributions to the discussion in traditional scholarly outlets have so far been rare. This book aims to bridge the gap between scientific rigor and practical utility.

My heartfelt thanks go above all to my family: to my wife Friederike and my children Frida and Anton, who had to do without me on many evenings because of this book. Many thanks also to Leonardo Milla for editing and constructive support, as well as to Celina Wendler for her energetic assistance as a student assistant and her helpful feedback on the manuscript. Finally, a thank you to my students, who showed great patience with my digressions on the topic of AI during the summer semester of 2025.

AI is not only the subject of this book, but was also extensively used in its creation—from the initial idea through research and development to the final review. In particular, models from OpenAI (GPT 4o, GPT-4.1, GPT-4.5, o3, o4-mini-high), Anthropic (Sonnet 3.7, 4.0), and Google (Gemini Flash 2.5, Pro 2.5) were employed. However, responsibility for the content, oversight, and scientific contextualization always remained with me.

I wish all readers an inspiring read and much curiosity, courage, and joy as you explore the possibilities presented.

Hanover, Germany
July 2025

Fabian Lang

Contents

List of Abbreviations

AGI	Artificial General Intelligence
AI	Artificial Intelligence
ALLEA	All European Academies
APA	American Psychological Association
BMI	Body Mass Index
BPMN	Business Process Model and Notation
CoN	Chain-of-Note
CoT	Chain-of-Thought
CoT-SC	Chain-of-Thought Self-Consistency
CoVe	Chain of Verification
DFG	German Research Foundation
DOI	Digital Object Identifier
EU	European Union
ERA	European Research Area Platform
GPT	Generative Pre-trained Transformer
HEPI	Higher Education Policy Institute
HTML	Hypertext Markup Language
ICL	In-Context Learning
JSON	JavaScript Object Notation
LLM	Large Language Model
LRM	Large Reasoning Model
NLP	Natural Language Processing
PDF	Portable Document Format
RAG	Retrieval-Augmented Generation
RaR	Rephrase and Respond
SVG	Scalable Vector Graphics
ToT	Tree-of-Thoughts
VIF	Variance Inflation Factor
XML	Extensible Markup Language

List of Figures

List of Tables

Prompt Directory

Introduction: Intelligent Machines Are Changing the World

1

Abstract

Artificial intelligence (AI) is fundamentally transforming university studies and is increasingly becoming an integral part of academic work processes. The introductory chapter describes this transformation and highlights the opportunities, challenges, and uncertainties that arise for students and instructors. It illustrates how widespread the use of generative AI already is, the potential it holds for learning and academic work, and which competencies will be particularly in demand in the future. At the same time, it becomes clear that clear guidelines, institutional support, and didactic concepts are often lacking. These gaps lead to uncertainty in dealing with AI and raise questions about academic integrity, responsibility, and transparency. The chapter therefore emphasizes the need for a structural and cultural framework for the reflective use of AI in higher education. Against this background, the book positions itself as a practical guide that supports both students and instructors in the competent use of AI applications such as ChatGPT and provides orientation for the responsible use of AI in academic work.

"Technology is neither good nor bad; nor is it neutral."
– First Kranzberg Law (Kranzberg, 1995, p. 5)

1.1 Transformation of Academic Study Through AI

Artificial Intelligence (AI), particularly in the form of chatbots such as ChatGPT, Claude, or Copilot, has rapidly become a defining tool in everyday academic life. A recent survey by the UK Higher Education Policy Institute (HEPI) demonstrates this rapid rise: while in 2023 only about two-thirds of students used generative AI, by the end of 2024 the figure had already reached 92%. The areas of application

F. Lang, *Using Artificial Intelligence in Term Papers and Theses*,
https://doi.org/10.1007/978-3-662-73208-3_1

are diverse, as students use AI not only to compose texts, but also to, among other things, prepare complex content in an understandable way, summarize scholarly articles, develop ideas for research questions, or sharpen their arguments (Freeman, 2025).

Meta-analyses show that the use of AI in education, primarily in higher education, can significantly improve learning outcomes and also has a positive impact on attitudes toward learning (Dong et al., 2025; Tlili et al., 2025; Wang & Fan, 2025). The studies indicate that AI support is particularly effective when integrated into problem-based or reflective learning concepts. The greatest impact is achieved when AI is used in the role of an intelligent tutor—that is, when the technology provides targeted guidance, feedback, and support throughout the individual learning process (Wang & Fan, 2025).

These developments show that confident use of AI has already become a key competency in academic study. Furthermore, the reflective use of AI tools is among the most important future skills for professional practice. In a recent survey of employers, competencies in AI and Big Data were rated as the fastest-growing qualifications. 88% of respondents expect these skills to become significantly more important within the next five years (World Economic Forum, 2025). Students therefore need not only to specialize in their subject areas, but also to learn how to use AI technologies confidently and critically. AI competence is not merely an additional technical skill, but is increasingly becoming an integral part of academic education.

But this is precisely where a significant gap becomes apparent. Despite high usage rates, according to the HEPI study, only about a quarter of students feel encouraged or supported by their university in using AI (Freeman, 2025). Surveys of university staff paint a similarly ambivalent picture regarding AI: about one fifth of respondents report approaching AI with great or very great caution, while a quarter express an enthusiastic or very enthusiastic attitude (Robert & McCormack, 2025). Despite this range of opinions, most instructors overall view AI more as an opportunity than a risk (Rong & Chun, 2025). At the same time, a clear majority of instructors also see serious risks, particularly with regard to possible misinformation, data protection issues, and potential for misuse (Robert & McCormack, 2025). While more than half of instructors already use AI primarily for preparing their own teaching, most do so only to a limited or moderate extent (Rong & Chun, 2025). In addition to individual skepticism, institutional change at universities is also progressing slowly. In many places, there is still a lack of adequate AI tools, binding guidelines, and professional development opportunities for instructors (Robert & McCormack, 2025).

This combination of individual reservations and lack of institutional anchoring leads to noticeable uncertainty—both among instructors and students. While some instructors use AI applications purposefully and recognize their potential, many remain unclear about which forms of use are permissible, meaningful, or even desired. Above all, the lack of organizational regulations and missing sociocultural context, such as peer influence, are barriers to acceptance for instructors (Ofosu-Ampong, 2024). Students, in turn, often operate in a gray area: they use AI tools but do not know whether this aligns with their university's expectations or complies with the rules of good academic practice. This uncertainty can lead to a sense of moral unease, i.e., a feeling of doing something not quite right, even though no explicit rule has been broken. This phenomenon is also referred to as "AI guilt" (Chan, 2024). Without clear guidance, didactic framing, and institutional support, a field of tension arises that is more likely to hinder than to promote productive developments.

The task for universities in the future is therefore to create the structural and cultural framework for a responsible and competency-oriented approach to AI. The aim is to develop binding guidelines that uphold academic integrity while also recognizing and harnessing the potential of AI technologies (Ren & Wu, 2025; Wu et al., 2024).

At the same time, didactic concepts must be developed that regard AI not only as a tool, but also as an object of academic reflection. Instructors need professional development opportunities and practical resources to confidently integrate AI into their teaching practice. Finally, students should be specifically empowered to use AI competently, creatively, and critically.

AI chatbots open up new possibilities for academic work, but their effective use requires more than just technical skills: what is crucial is the ability to critically reflect on the use of such technologies, to contextualize their results, and to use them in accordance with academic standards. In other words: the use of AI demands a high degree of responsibility. This means that the technology must not become a substitute for academic thinking, but must be used in such a way that humans retain control, ensure quality, and take responsibility for the results.

This is precisely where this book comes in: it is aimed primarily at students, but also at instructors, and seeks to provide a practice-oriented guide for the reflective use of AI in academic work. At the same time, it aims to raise awareness of the associated challenges and to offer a critical perspective that helps to safeguard academic integrity when dealing with new technologies.

1.2 Understanding This Book

The term Artificial Intelligence (AI) is often used imprecisely and very broadly in everyday language. This book also deliberately refrains from a strictly scientific definition—for the sake of clarity. When AI is referred to here, it is meant in the narrower sense of generative AI systems based on so-called large language models (LLMs). These models are capable of generating human-like text, responding to complex queries, and communicating in a dialog-oriented manner.

The focus is not on specialized AI applications that fully automate individual processes such as literature searches or statistical analyses. Instead, the emphasis is on generally accessible AI chat systems such as ChatGPT, Claude, Microsoft Copilot, or open platforms based on architectures like Llama, DeepSeek, or Qwen. What characterizes these systems is their operability via natural language—a feature that makes them usable even for non-technical users and enables a wide range of applications in academic life.

A central aim of this book is to teach practical use of these AI systems in academic work processes. To this end, numerous example prompts are presented, specifically related to academic papers and theses. These prompts can generally be used directly or adapted with minor modifications to suit one's own topics. At the same time, the examples provide a basic understanding of how effective prompts should be structured, the considerations underlying their formulation, and how this knowledge can be transferred to one's own needs. In this way, they not only promote direct application, but also the development of one's own, situation-appropriate prompts—a key competency for confident use of generative AI.

1.3 Structure of the Book

The book is divided into ten chapters, the structure of which is visualized in Fig. 1.1.

Following this introduction, Chap. 2 first addresses the technical foundations of large language models (LLMs). This chapter provides a basic understanding of how such models work, the principles underlying them, and the implications that arise from them. Building on this technical foundation, Chap. 3 covers so-called prompt engineering, i.e., techniques for formulating precise and effective inputs to obtain high-quality and meaningful results from an AI chatbot. Chap. 4 takes a closer look at the issue of academic integrity in the context of generative AI. It develops principles for responsible use and explains how the use of AI can be documented transparently and correctly.

The following chapters focus on practical application. Starting with Chap. 5, a practice-oriented guide is developed that systematically accompanies the individual phases of academic work. The focus is always on concrete uses of AI, each

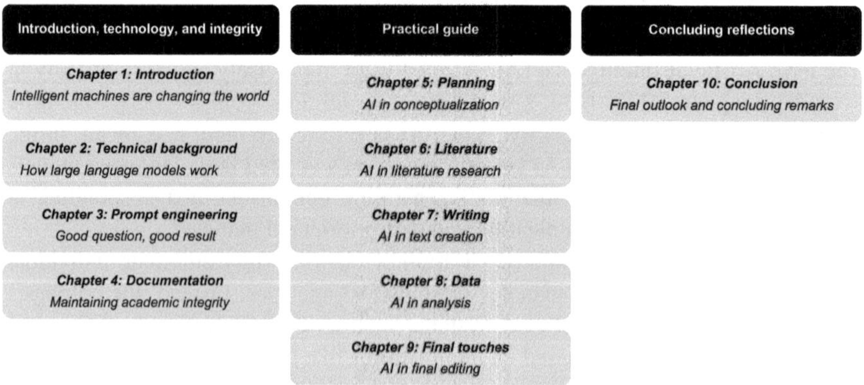

Fig. 1.1 Overview of the structure of the book (own illustration)

illustrated by example prompts and supplemented by critical reflection. Chap. 5 addresses the planning phase: it shows how AI can support topic selection, narrowing down, and the writing of a proposal. Chap. 6 is devoted to working with literature and presents ways to use AI to find, evaluate, and analyze relevant sources. The following Chap. 7 deals with text production. It examines how AI can be used to improve structure, language, and argumentation without undermining academic standards. Chap. 8 focuses on data collection and analysis, particularly in supporting methodological understanding as well as analysis, interpretation, and visualization. Finally, Chap. 9 centers on final editing and shows how AI can be effectively used for linguistic and formal revision before submission.

The book concludes with Chap. 10. It situates AI within technological change, reflects on future developments, and summarizes the book's key findings in a conclusion.

References

Chan, C. K. Y. (2024). *Exploring the factors of "AI guilt" among students—are you guilty of using AI in your homework?*. https://arxiv.org/abs/2407.10777v1.

Dong, L., Tang, X., & Wang, X. (2025). Examining the effect of artificial intelligence in relation to students' academic achievement: A meta-analysis. *Computers and Education: Artificial Intelligence, 8*, 100400. https://doi.org/10.1016/j.caeai.2025.100400.

Freeman, J. (2025). *Student generative AI survey 2025.* HEPI Policy Note 61.

Kranzberg, M. (1995). Technology and history: "Kranzberg's Laws". *Bulletin of Science, Technology & Society, 15*(1), 5–13. https://doi.org/10.1177/027046769501500104.

Ofosu-Ampong, K. (2024). Beyond the hype: Exploring faculty perceptions and acceptability of AI in teaching practices. *Discover Education, 3*(1). https://doi.org/10.1007/s44217-024-00128-4.

Ren, X., & Wu, M. L. (2025). Examining teaching competencies and challenges while integrating artificial intelligence in higher education. *TechTrends, 69*(3), 519–538. https://doi.org/10.1007/s11528-025-01055-3.

Robert, J., & McCormack, M. (2025, 26. Juni). *2025 AI landscape study: Into the digital AI divide.* EDUCAUSE. https://library.educause.edu/resources/2025/2/2025-educause-ai-landscape-study.

Rong, H., & Chun, C. (2025). *Digital Education Council global AI faculty survey 2025.* Digital Education Council.

Tlili, A., Saqer, K., Salha, S., & Huang, R. (2025). Investigating the effect of artificial intelligence in education (AIEd) on learning achievement: A meta-analysis and research synthesis. *Information Development, 41*(3), 825–842. https://doi.org/10.1177/02666669241304407.

Wang, J., & Fan, W. (2025). The effect of ChatGPT on students' learning performance, learning perception, and higher-order thinking: Insights from a meta-analysis. *Humanities and Social Sciences Communications, 12*(1). https://doi.org/10.1057/s41599-025-04787-y.

World Economic Forum. (2025, 26. Juni). *Future of jobs report 2025.* https://www.weforum.org/publications/the-future-of-jobs-report-2025/.

Wu, C., Zhang, H., & Carroll, J. M. (2024). *AI governance in higher education: Case studies of guidance at big ten universities.*. https://doi.org/10.48550/arXiv.2409.02017.

Technical Background: Large Language Models (LLM)

2

Abstract

This chapter provides a fundamental overview of how large language models (LLMs) work and systematically situates them within the broader field of artificial intelligence. It explains key concepts such as tokenization, embedding, attention, and sampling, and describes how models like ChatGPT generate linguistic outputs based on statistical probabilities. The underlying transformer architecture is described step by step and its relevance for text processing is discussed. In addition, central technical limitations such as context length, hallucinations, bias, and lack of a genuine world understanding are addressed. It is made clear that, despite their high expressive power, LLMs still constitute weak AI, as they lack conscious understanding. The aim of the chapter is to provide students with a technical foundation for understanding how these systems work—as a basis for reflective and responsible use in academic work, even without prior technical knowledge. This includes the ability to comprehend key concepts, assess capabilities, and critically recognize system-related limitations.

"All models are wrong."
– George E. P. Box (1976, p. 792)

2.1 What is AI?

In everyday language, the term artificial intelligence (AI) is often used imprecisely and serves as an umbrella term for a wide range of technologies—from simple automations to learning systems. At its core, however, AI is about machines that exhibit abilities typically understood as expressions of intelligence: problem-solving, learning, planning, reasoning, etc. But what makes a machine intelligent in this sense? And how can intelligence even be defined?

F. Lang, *Using Artificial Intelligence in Term Papers and Theses*,
https://doi.org/10.1007/978-3-662-73208-3_2

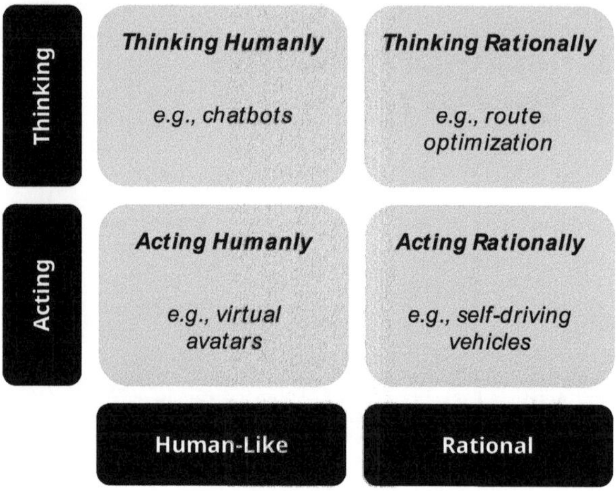

Fig. 2.1 Dimensions of artificial intelligence, based on Russell and Norvig (2023)

An influential framework for classifying artificial intelligence comes from Russell and Norvig (2023). They classify AI along two central dimensions: the reference frame of intelligence and the type of intelligence. The model is shown in Fig. 2.1.

The first dimension, the reference frame, asks what intelligence is oriented toward. On the one hand, a machine can be designed to act in a human-like way. It then imitates, for example, language or problem-solving strategies as observed in humans. On the other hand, a machine can be designed to act formally and logically rational. This distinction is significant, because while human behavior is considered intelligent, it is strongly shaped by psychological factors, social context, and cognitive heuristics, and thus is not consistently rational in the strictly mathematical-logical sense.

The second dimension concerns the type of intelligence, i.e., the question of what is to be achieved intelligently. Here, a distinction is made between systems focused on thinking and those that emphasize acting. Intelligent thinking includes abilities such as reasoning, planning, and learning, i.e., it is about the cognitive processing of information. Intelligent acting, on the other hand, refers to externally observable behavior. The system not only makes internal decisions but also implements them in a defined environment.

As this theoretical framework makes clear, the term artificial intelligence extends far beyond the functioning and scope of large language models (LLMs) such as ChatGPT, Claude, or Copilot. While large language models are undoubtedly a form of AI, the converse is not true: not all intelligent systems are based on language models. AI is a broad field of research and application that encompasses numerous paradigms, methods, and objectives.

A central role within this field is played by machine learning. These are methods in which systems are not explicitly programmed but independently derive structures, patterns, and solutions from available data or observations. The goal is to develop a model that learns from examples and can then make generalizable decisions or predictions.

A particularly powerful and now widely used subfield of machine learning is deep learning. Deep learning systems are based on artificial neural networks consisting of many interconnected layers. Unlike classical learning methods, where human experts define relevant features, deep learning models learn these features themselves, provided sufficiently large datasets are available. The models independently prioritize those features that are particularly relevant for the given task.

LLMs fall precisely into this category: they are deep learning models trained on massive text corpora using neural networks. Their "understanding" of language is not based on semantic rules or lexical knowledge, but on the statistical recognition and weighted processing of linguistic patterns across many layers. In this sense, LLMs are not only a concrete manifestation of AI, but also a specific example of machine learning and, within that, the subfield of deep learning. At the same time, large language models also belong to the subfield of generative AI—that is, the class of intelligent systems designed to autonomously generate new content. This includes, among other things, the creation of texts, images, audio files, or videos. Generative AI is not primarily based on content analysis or classification, but uses learned patterns to produce corresponding outputs.

Artificial intelligence as a field of research and application therefore encompasses far more than just LLMs. For example, symbolic AI, expert systems, robotic applications, or simulation-based decision-making procedures are also included, some of which are based on completely different principles. Figure 2.2 (see, e.g., Jeong, 2024 or Pressman et al., 2024) illustrates this classification and shows how large language models can be systematically located within the overall field of AI.

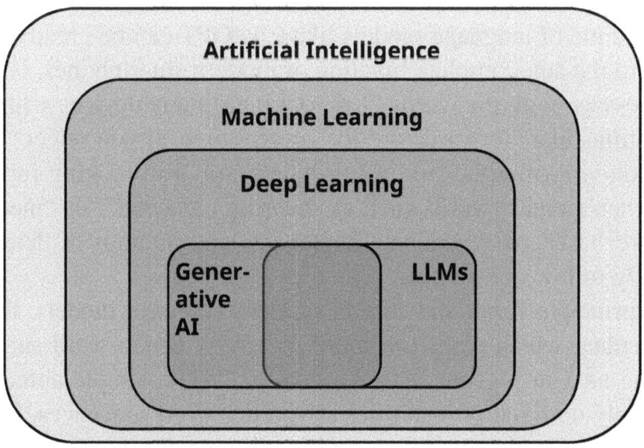

Fig. 2.2 Classification of LLMs within the AI fields, after Jeong (2024)

A common classification of AI systems is based on the distinction between weak and strong artificial intelligence according to Searle (1980).

Weak AI refers to systems that merely simulate cognitive processes without possessing true understanding or consciousness. These systems are primarily designed as tools: they solve defined tasks within a given framework, often using fixed rules or trained models. Language processing systems, chatbots, or recommendation systems typically fall into this category. Even large language models, despite their impressive expressive capabilities, belong to this class, as they generate language based on statistical patterns, not on genuine understanding or intentional thought.

Strong AI—or artificial general intelligence (AGI)—by contrast, would possess actual consciousness, i.e., it could not only generate language or solve problems, but also understand, reflect, and act intentionally. A strong AI would be capable of independent learning in open, dynamic contexts and could flexibly adapt to new, unstructured situations, much like a human. This would not be about imitating intelligent behavior, but about the existence of internal mental states such as beliefs, intentions, or feelings. Such an AI would be highly adaptable and could independently solve a wide variety of problem classes without human assistance. As a hypothetical extension of this idea, a third stage of development is often discussed: so-called superintelligence (Good, 1965). This refers to a form of artificial intelligence that not only matches but vastly surpasses human cognitive abilities in almost all dimensions.

Despite the significant advances in large language models, it should be noted: strong AI does not yet exist. Systems like ChatGPT mark a new level of functional capability within weak AI, but they merely simulate thought processes without executing them consciously. How language models actually work and the mechanisms behind them will be explained later in this chapter.

2.2 The Fundamental Idea Behind Generative Models

The basic principle of language models like ChatGPT can be greatly simplified by comparing it to the autocomplete function of modern smartphones. For example, if you start a message with the words "I'm looking," many devices will suggest suitable continuations like "forward" or "for" in real time. If you select "forward," the next suggestion will often be "to". After the phrase "I'm looking forward to", the system may then suggest words such as "hearing", "seeing", or "meeting". These predictions are based on statistical frequencies and attempt to determine which words typically follow one another.

This very principle forms the core of modern language models: they also continuously calculate which word (or, more precisely, which word subunit) is most likely to come next in a given sentence context. While simple autocomplete systems usually rely on fixed probabilities or smaller word sequences, large language models analyze entire paragraphs, sections, or even the entire preceding text to generate context-sensitive and flexible continuations. The text is generated step by step, word by word. This creates the impression of "intelligent" answers, even though the model is only predicting probabilities and continuing linguistic patterns.

The importance of context can be illustrated well with a simple example: If a sentence begins with "In Germany, people eat …," the language model calculates a probability for each possible next word—based on what frequently followed in similar situations in the training data. If the sentence stands alone, the following continuations are possible, among others (probabilities are fictitious):

- traditionally (25% probability)
  e.g., "… traditionally often dishes like sauerkraut, bratwurst, and potatoes."
- many (15% probability)
  e.g., "… many different kinds of food, as many cuisines from around the world are popular."
- fresh (10% probability)
  e.g., "… fresh bread, meat, and regional specialties."
- often (5% probability)
  e.g., "… at home, but also in bakeries or restaurants."

The most likely next word in our example is "traditionally." If this is selected, the model then calculates the most probable continuation—here, for example, "often." This process is repeated step by step: for each new word, a probability distribution is calculated based on the preceding context. The text is thus generated word by word, without the model knowing from the outset how the sentence or paragraph will end. Only when a meaningful linguistic unit is reached, such as a period, the end of a paragraph, or a logical conclusion, does this process end.

The answers here primarily revolve around what foods Germans typically consume. If we now introduce additional context and imagine the text begins with the sentence "In Spain, people rarely eat dinner before 8 p.m. In Germany, people eat …," then the next word or sentence ending might look like this:

- early (40% probability)
  e.g., "… early, usually between 6 and 7 p.m."
- late (10% probability)
  e.g., "… late, but usually before 9 p.m."
- together (5% probability)
  e.g., "… together at the family table."
- outside (3% probability)
  e.g., "… outside, often in a beer garden."

The changed context significantly shifts the generated continuations: instead of focusing on what is eaten, the emphasis is now on when and how people eat. This example shows how sensitively language models respond to the context provided to them. They make their decisions not only based on individual words, but also incorporate content relationships to generate a plausible and coherent continuation.

2.3 How Large Language Models (LLMs) Work

This chapter provides a fundamental overview of how large language models function, how their architecture is structured, and the way in which they generate linguistic output. It explains key concepts such as tokenization, embedding, attention, and sampling, while also highlighting the limitations and challenges that arise from the technology. The aim is to provide a solid understanding of how these models work—as a basis for reflective and responsible use in academic contexts.

For those who wish to dive deeper into the technological and mathematical foundations, the following works are recommended:

Wolfram (2023): *What Is ChatGPT Doing... and Why Does It Work?*

- Provides an in-depth, accessible, and practical explanation of the technological and mathematical structure of ChatGPT and similar models, making complex processes understandable through concrete examples
- Recommended for anyone seeking further, easily accessible background information after the concise introduction in this book

Kamath et al. (2024): *Large Language Models: A Deep Dive – Bridging Theory and Practice.*

- Systematically and comprehensively presents the theoretical and mathematical foundations of modern LLMs
- Especially suitable for advanced students and researchers seeking an in-depth understanding of the mathematical and technological foundations of LLMs

2.3.1 The Transformer Architecture

The core of modern language models such as ChatGPT is the so-called transformer architecture. This is a specialized form of deep learning originally developed for tasks in the field of natural language processing (NLP), but which is now also widely used in other areas such as computer vision, speech processing, or specialized scientific domains (Lin et al., 2022). The transformer architecture is based on a modular structure and is essentially divided into four successive layers that together enable the processing and generation of text (see Fig. 2.3).

In the tokenizer, the input text is first broken down into smaller units—so-called tokens. This segmentation allows the language model to flexibly handle different word forms. It does not need to know every possible word variant separately, but can recognize variants of the same word stem by combining individual tokens.

The next step is embedding, i.e., the numerical representation of the tokens. Each token is translated into a vector of numbers. These vectors form the basis for all further computations in the model: They make language mathematically

2.3.4 Transformation: Recognizing Context

Embedding enables the language model to capture certain semantic and syntactic properties and to recognize similarities between words. However, this is context-independent. This limitation becomes clear with ambiguous words: A word like "bat" always receives the same vector in a static embedding—regardless of whether it refers to an animal or a piece of sports equipment. However, the surrounding context makes the intended meaning clear: "at dusk, the bat..."or "in baseball, the bat...".

To capture the context of a word, modern AI language models use a central innovation: the attention mechanism. This method for transformer models was first introduced in the groundbreaking and widely cited paper "Attention is All You Need" by Vaswani et al. (2017). Attention is considered the secret ingredient behind the power of today's transformer models.

At its core, attention means that when processing a text, each individual token is not only considered in isolation, but in relation to all other tokens in the given context. The model analyzes which other tokens are particularly relevant for interpreting a specific token and weights them accordingly. This creates a dynamic, context-dependent representation of meaning.

A simple example illustrates how this works: In the sentence "The cat ate the mouse because it was hungry," the pronoun "it" refers to the cat. In the sentence "The cat ate the mouse because it was tasty," the context suggests that "it" refers to the mouse. Without a mechanism like attention, such nuances of meaning would be difficult to resolve. Through this targeted context analysis, the model can thus differentiate between ambiguities and follow grammatical rules for sentence structure.

Figure 2.7 illustrates how the attention mechanism works in a language model using an example. The sample sentence is: "The developer team fixes the program, as it is faulty." The graphic shows, for selected tokens ("it", "program", and "team"), the distribution of attention to other tokens in the sentence (the highest attention values are highlighted in color).

A key feature is that each of these tokens initially directs high attention to itself—a typical behavior of language models that serves stability and self-localization in the sentence. Particularly interesting, however, is the attention of "it": Here, it can be seen that the model focuses on "program" and its article "the." This weighting suggests that "it" in this case correctly refers to "program." At the same time, "faulty" is also given increased attention, as it provides the substantive statement about the pronoun.

"Program" also shows characteristic patterns: As the object of the main clause, its relationship to the verb ("corrects") and to the subject ("team") is made visible by increased attention. This reflects the syntactic structure of the sentence and shows how the model recognizes the distribution of roles.

For "team," in turn, it is evident that the compound subject "developer team" is held together by attention. The model thus recognizes that it is a single unit, even though the word consists of several components.

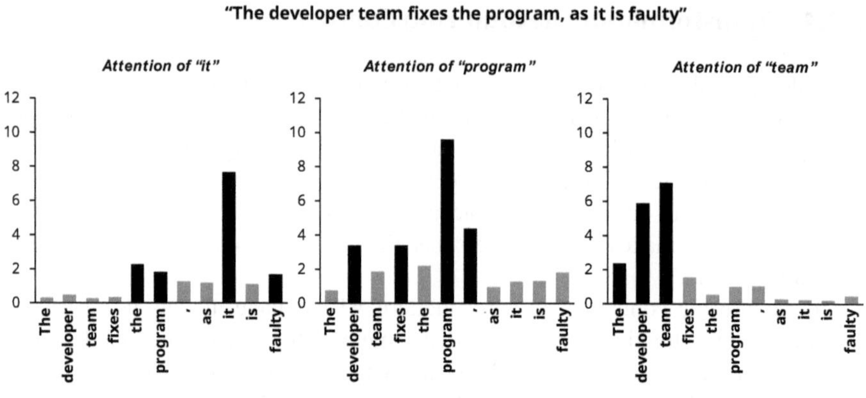

Fig. 2.7 Example of attention values

This example clearly demonstrates how powerful the attention mechanism is in capturing syntactic and semantic relationships. It allows the model to identify context-dependent references, resolve meanings correctly, and thus develop a consistent interpretation of complex sentences.

2.3.5 Decoding: Back to Output

As a result of processing in the transformer layers, a so-called score—a numerical value expressing how much the model trusts each possible next token in the given context—is generated for every possible next token. These scores are not yet probabilities in the strict sense, but raw values that are converted into a probability distribution in the next step. This is done during the model's decoding using a softmax function, which maps all scores to values between 0 and 1 and ensures that their sum is exactly 1. This creates a probability distribution from which the model selects the most likely next token, or, under certain settings, deliberately allows less likely variants to encourage variation and creativity.

Figure 2.8 shows an example of such a probability distribution, using words instead of tokens for better understanding. In the example, it is assumed that one word ("The") has already been generated.

A seemingly obvious but in practice unsatisfactory strategy would be to always select the most likely next token. This approach—known as greedy decoding—results in generated texts that are predictable, monotonous, and often stylistically lacking in variety. The model's expressiveness and creativity are thus greatly limited.

To counteract this, modern language models use so-called sampling methods. Instead of always choosing the most likely token, the model randomly selects from a set of plausible alternatives—the sample—based on their respective probabilities. The model thus generates variations by sampling from possible continuations. Two of the most commonly used sampling strategies are top-k sampling and top-p sampling (the latter also known as nucleus sampling).

In top-k sampling, the selection is limited to the k most likely tokens. For example, if $k = 3$ is set, the model chooses only from the three tokens with the highest probabilities and makes a random decision within this selection based on the respective probabilities. This reduces the risk of rare or irrelevant tokens being chosen, but still maintains some variation.

A disadvantage of the top-k method becomes apparent when the probability distribution is flat: In that case, a meaningful token might be in fourth or fifth place and still be excluded. This is where top-p sampling comes in. Instead of using a fixed number of candidates, the model sums the probabilities of the tokens until a predetermined threshold p (for example, 50%) is exceeded. The selection thus does not always include the same number of tokens, but those that together cover a certain cumulative probability. Here, too, the final selection is random. Figure 2.9 illustrates the two methods using the previous example.

During decoding, the behavior of a language model can be specifically influenced. In addition to sampling methods such as top-k and top-p, another key parameter plays a role here: the so-called temperature.

Temperature acts directly on the probability distribution of potential next tokens. More precisely, it controls how strongly the model adheres to the calculated probabilities. A low temperature leads to a steeper distribution: The most likely tokens are disproportionately favored, while less likely candidates are devalued. The model thus becomes more focused and deterministic. This results in higher content precision and lower error rates, but at the expense of stylistic variety.

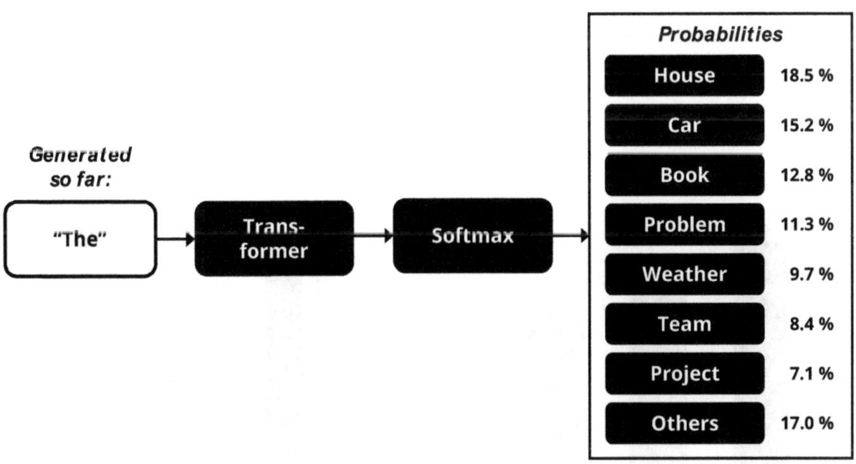

Fig. 2.8 Sample probability distribution

In contrast, a high temperature flattens the distribution: Differences in probabilities are smoothed out, and even rarer tokens have more chances. This increases linguistic variety and can lead to surprising, creative, or unconventional responses. At the same time, however, the risk of vagueness or factual inaccuracies also increases. At a temperature of 1, the proportions remain unchanged.

Figure 2.10 shows, by way of example, the influence of different temperature settings on an identical initial distribution: At T = 0.25, the selection is clearly focused on the most likely token. At T = 1.5, however, the probabilities are distributed almost evenly across several alternatives. This control allows the model's behavior to be specifically modulated depending on the application scenario, for example, between factual clarity and creative openness.

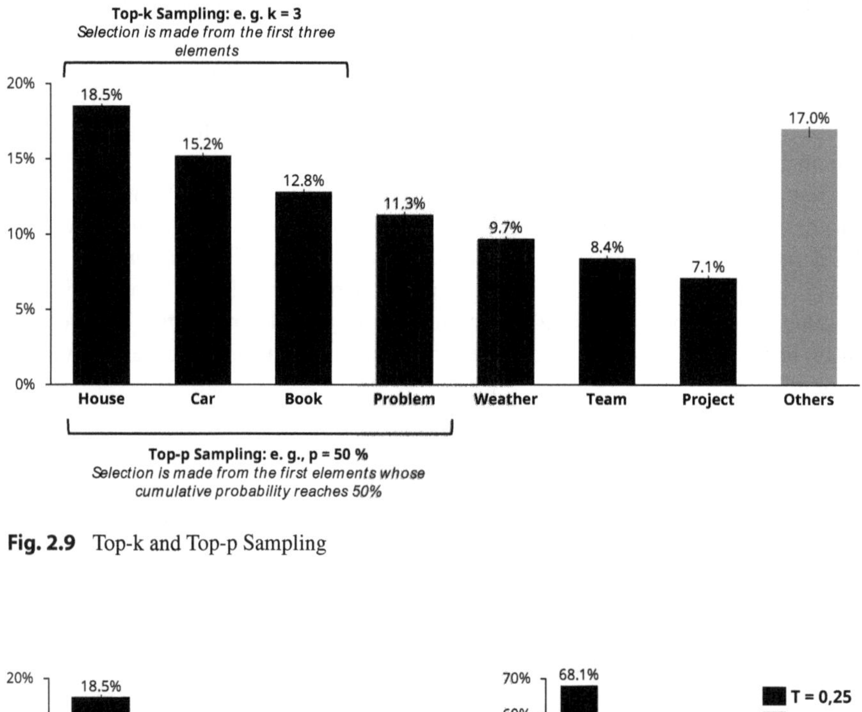

Fig. 2.9 Top-k and Top-p Sampling

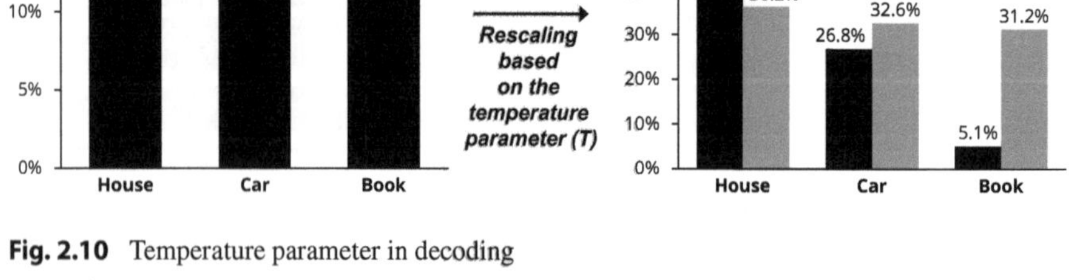

Fig. 2.10 Temperature parameter in decoding

2.4 Illusion of Thinking and Technical Limitations

The explained functioning and architecture of language models give rise to a number of inherent weaknesses and system-related limitations that should be critically reflected upon when using them.

As explained, LLMs are not based on **understanding**, but on the calculation of statistical probabilities within linguistic patterns they have learned during training. Even though their responses often appear coherent, purposeful, and seemingly "intelligent," these models possess neither consciousness nor a mental model of the world. They simulate language through mathematical pattern recognition, which humans mistake for "thinking." Genuine cognitive engagement does not take place (Venkatasubramanian, 2025).

Another problem is the possibility of so-called **hallucinations**. These occur when the model generates factually incorrect but linguistically plausible information—such as when it encounters gaps in its training, overextends the context, or selects an inappropriate token during decoding (Huang et al., 2025). Such hallucinated statements are particularly problematic in scientific contexts, as they may appear to be reliable information without clear citation or verification.

There is also the knowledge limitation of the models (**knowledge cutoff**): LLMs are based exclusively on the state of the data available to them at the time of training. Current events or developments after that point are, in principle, unknown to them (Li et al., 2025). While newer systems can retrospectively retrieve information by accessing external sources such as the internet or search engines, this capability still depends on the model architecture and the specific application conditions.

The question of creative **originality** also deserves critical consideration. Language models generate seemingly new content by recombining already known linguistic patterns. This statistical recombination gives the illusion of creativity, but is not a creative act in the true sense. The model does not "invent," but produces variations of what is already known. While this is often impressive, it is not original, that is, genuinely new (Franceschelli & Musolesi, 2025).

Another common misconception concerns the use of language models for **mathematical calculations or logical tasks**. Since LLMs are based on linguistic tokens and not on numerical operations, errors frequently occur (Qian et al., 2023). An illustrative example is the so-called "strawberry problem": If the model is asked how many times the letter "r" appears in "strawberry," it often fails. This is because the model does not process the word as a sequence of letters, but as a token ID or vector—the letters themselves are not part of its internal representation. Accordingly, the prerequisites for accurate counting or complex calculations are lacking, unless additional tools such as programming code are used (Fu et al., 2024).

Finally, **context processing** by LLMs is also limited. The size of the attention matrix is technically constrained. For very long texts or extended dialogues, this can lead to loss of context: earlier information drops out of the memory area and is no longer adequately considered (Fei et al., 2024). In addition, as text length increases, precision suffers due to the influence of irrelevant content, which acts as noise and distorts attention. The larger the context, the more difficult it becomes for the model to correctly establish relevant connections (Liu et al., 2024).

Because language models are trained on large amounts of text data, they not only adopt linguistic patterns and semantic structures, but also **biases** and stereotypes contained therein. These are not explicitly labeled in the training data, but are often deeply embedded in the language, for example through unbalanced representations, stereotypical role models, or discriminatory formulations. If certain narratives or stereotypes are overrepresented in the training data, this is directly reflected in the model's responses. For example, a gender bias can arise in job titles (e.g., by implicitly portraying engineers als male and nurses as female), or cultural, ethnic, or social prejudices may be unconsciously reproduced (Kotek et al., 2023). This is referred to as algorithmic bias (Kordzadeh & Ghasemaghaei, 2022).

These limitations are not accidental, but a direct expression of the underlying technology. They result from the way language models are trained and constructed—statistically, data-driven, and without genuine understanding. Responsible and reflective use of LLMs therefore requires leveraging their impressive capabilities in a targeted manner, without losing sight of their system-related limitations. Only those who make this distinction can use the technology meaningfully, critically, and competently in scientific contexts.

References

Box, G. E. P. (1976). Science and statistics. *Journal of the American Statistical Association, 71*(356), 791–799.

Fei, W., Niu, X., Zhou, P., Hou, L., Bai, B., Deng, L., & Han, W. (2024). Extending context window of Large Language Models via semantic compression. In L.-W. Ku, A. Martins, & V. Srikumar (Eds.), *Findings of the Association for Computational Linguistics ACL 2024* (pp. 5169–5181). Association for Computational Linguistics). https://doi.org/10.18653/v1/2024.findings-acl.306.

Franceschelli, G., & Musolesi, M. (2025). On the creativity of Large Language Models. *AI & SOCIETY, 40*(5), 3785–3795. https://doi.org/10.1007/s00146-024-02127-3.

Fu, T., Ferrando, R., Conde, J., Arriaga, C., & Reviriego, P. (2024). *Why do large language models (LLMs) struggle to count letters?*. https://arxiv.org/abs/2412.18626v1.

Good, I. J. (1965). Speculations concerning the first ultraintelligent machine. *Advances in Computers, 6*, 31–88. https://doi.org/10.1016/S0065-2458(08)60418-0.

Huang, L., Yu, W., Ma, W., Zhong, W., Feng, Z., Wang, H., Chen, Q., Peng, W., Feng, X., Qin, B., & Liu, T. (2025). A survey on hallucination in Large Language Models: Principles, taxonomy, challenges, and open questions. *ACM Transactions on Information Systems, 43*(2), 1–55. https://doi.org/10.1145/3703155.

Hugging Face. (2025, 6. Juni). *Llama4*. https://huggingface.co/docs/transformers/en/model_doc/llama4.

Jeong, C. (2024). Fine-tuning and utilization methods of domain-specific LLMs. *Journal of Intelligence and Information Systems, 30*(1), 93–120.

Kamath, U., Keenan, K., Somers, G., & Sorenson, S. (2024). *Large Language Models: A deep dive: Bridging theory and practice* (1st ed. 2024). Springer. https://doi.org/10.1007/978-3-031-65647-7.

Kordzadeh, N., & Ghasemaghaei, M. (2022). Algorithmic bias: Review, synthesis, and future research directions. *European Journal of Information Systems, 31*(3), 388–409. https://doi.org/10.1080/0960085X.2021.1927212.

Kotek, H., Dockum, R., & Sun, D. (2023). Gender bias and stereotypes in Large Language Models. In M. Bernstein, S. Savage, & A. Bozzon (Eds.), *Proceedings of The ACM collective intelligence conference* (pp. 12–24). ACM. https://doi.org/10.1145/3582269.3615599.

Li, M., Zhao, Y., Zhang, W., Li, S., Xie, W., Ng, S.-K., Chua, T.-S., & Deng, Y. (2025). Knowledge boundary of large language models: A survey. In *63rd Annual Meeting of the Association for Computational Linguistics (ACL 2025).*

Lin, T., Wang, Y., Liu, X., & Qiu, X. (2022). A survey of transformers. *AI Open, 3*, 111–132. https://doi.org/10.1016/j.aiopen.2022.10.001.

Liu, N. F., Lin, K., Hewitt, J., Paranjape, A., Bevilacqua, M., Petroni, F., & Liang, P. (2024). Lost in the middle: How language models use long contexts. *Transactions of the Association for Computational Linguistics, 12*, 157–173. https://doi.org/10.1162/tacl_a_00638.

Pressman, S. M., Borna, S., Gomez-Cabello, C. A., Haider, S. A., Haider, C. R., & Forte, A. J. (2024). Clinical and surgical applications of Large Language Models: A systematic review. *Journal of Clinical Medicine, 13*(11). https://doi.org/10.3390/jcm13113041.

Qian, J., Wang, H., Li, Z., Li, S., & Yan, X. (2023). Limitations of language models in arithmetic and symbolic induction. In A. Rogers, J. Boyd-Graber & N. Okazaki (Eds.), *Proceedings of the 61st annual meeting of the Association for Computational Linguistics (Volume 1: Long Papers)* (pp. 9285–9298). Association for Computational Linguistics. https://doi.org/10.18653/v1/2023.acl-long.516.

Radford, A., Narasimhan, K., Salimans, T., & Sutskever, I. (2018, 6. Juni). Improving language understanding by generative pre-training. *OpenAI.* https://cdn.openai.com/research-covers/language-unsupervised/language_understanding_paper.pdf.

Russell, S. J., & Norvig, P. (2023). *Künstliche Intelligenz: Ein moderner Ansatz* (4., akt. ed.). Pearson.

Searle, J. R. (1980). Minds, brains, and programs. *Behavioral and Brain Sciences, 3*(3), 417–457.

Vaswani, A., Shazeer, N., Parmar, N., Uszkoreit, J., Jones, L., Gomez, A. N., Kaiser, L., & Polosukhin, I. (2017). *Attention is all you need.* https://arxiv.org/abs/1706.03762v5.

Venkatasubramanian, V. (2025). Do Large Language Models "understand" their knowledge? *AICHE Journal, 71*(3), Article e18661. https://doi.org/10.1002/aic.18661.

Wolfram, S. (2023). *What Is ChatGPT Doing... and Why Does It Work?* Wolfram Media.

References

3 Prompt Engineering: Good Question, Good Result

Abstract

This chapter provides a practice-oriented overview of prompt engineering for the targeted control of large language models in scientific contexts. It demonstrates how the structured design of prompts—through precise instructions, specific contexts, and clear requirements—improves the quality, relevance, and traceability of AI-generated responses. Methods are described that enable the model to understand tasks based on examples, analyze complex problems step by step, compare different solution approaches, and make its own reasoning process transparent. In addition, it explains how external information, verification steps, and the targeted parameterization of response style and length can further optimize results. The chapter also examines the role of integrated tools such as internet search, code generation, and agent-based workflows in expanding AI capabilities. A particular focus is placed on "prompting for prompts": in this approach, the AI itself is used to develop and optimize prompts. Overall, the chapter conveys the methodological foundations for the effective use of prompt engineering in scientific work.

"A prudent question is one-half of wisdom."
– Francis Bacon (quoted in Kessler & Bailey, 2007)

3.1 Concept and Delimitation of Prompt Engineering

The quality of interaction between humans and machines is crucial in determining the extent to which artificial intelligence (AI) can realize its potential in academic work. Especially when using large language models, the way a query—the so-called prompt—is formulated is decisive for the quality and accuracy of the

F. Lang, *Using Artificial Intelligence in Term Papers and Theses*,
https://doi.org/10.1007/978-3-662-73208-3_3

generated responses. Prompt engineering refers to the targeted design of these inputs to achieve the best possible results.

A prompt is an input command consisting of text or other data that provides an AI system, such as a large language model (LLM), with instructions or context to perform a specific task. The goal is to achieve the desired outcome through precise formulations. At the same time, it serves as the user interface for the LLM.

Prompt engineering, as well as the methods of transfer learning, fine tuning, and prompt tuning, make it possible to deploy a generally trained language model for specific tasks (see Fig. 3.1) (Patil & Gudivada, 2024; Sahoo et al., 2025).

Large language models are pre-trained on extensive datasets to capture a wide variety of linguistic patterns and relationships. However, to efficiently perform specialized tasks, a pre-trained base model can be adapted through fine tuning (see Fig. 3.1a). In fine tuning, the model parameters are specifically modified by adapting to a specialized dataset. This allows the model to acquire specific domain knowledge or adapt to particular linguistic requirements. This process enables a generally trained AI to be used more precisely and efficiently for individual tasks (Patil & Gudivada, 2024).

A more resource-efficient alternative to fine tuning is prompt tuning (see Fig. 3.1b). In prompt tuning, the base model remains unchanged, while each input is supplemented with a soft prompt. Unlike conventional text-based instructions, a soft prompt does not consist of natural language, but of a trainable numerical sequence. These numerical values influence the model's internal computations and steer response generation in a particular direction. In this way, the model can be adapted to specific tasks (Patil & Gudivada, 2024).

The simplest method to improve the quality of an AI-generated response, especially for users without programming knowledge, is prompt engineering (see Fig. 3.1c). Unlike fine-tuning or prompt tuning, which require deeper technical intervention, prompt engineering is based on deliberately optimizing the input prompt in order to obtain better and more relevant responses. In prompt engineering, not only the actual question or instruction is provided to the language model, but also additional contextual information and control instructions. These additional elements help the model better understand the intent of the request and

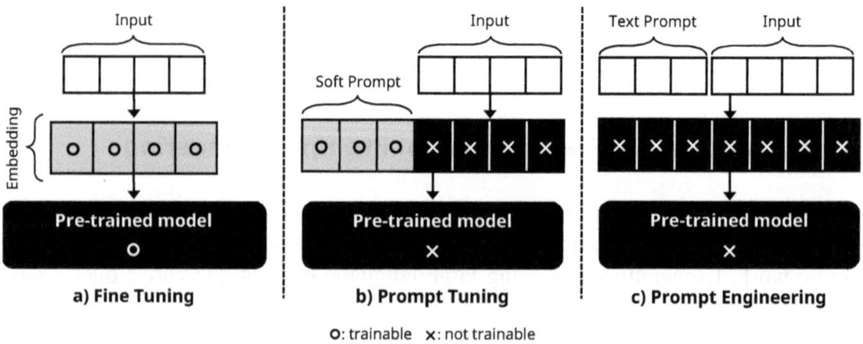

Fig. 3.1 Fine tuning, prompt tuning, and prompt engineering, after Shi and Lipani (2024)

generate a response that is more appropriate in terms of both content and style (Patil & Gudivada, 2024).

3.2 Anatomy of a Prompt

A prompt follows a specific structure that supports the model in interpreting the query. This subsection explains the essential components of a prompt and their functions.

3.2.1 Structure

A prompt is the input command with which an LLM is to perform a specific task. The quality of the prompt largely determines the precision and relevance of the AI-generated response.

The basic requirement for a prompt is a clear instruction to the AI that defines the task and the topic. In addition, two optional elements can be added to tailor the result to the individual wishes of the user: on the one hand, context, i.e., targeted additional information about the task, and on the other hand, specifications, i.e., requirements regarding the format, scope, or structure of the desired response (Giray, 2023; Zuckarelli, 2025). These two optional elements help to significantly improve the quality of AI responses. A schematic representation of the anatomy of a prompt can be found in Fig. 3.2, and an example of the three elements can be found in Prompt 3.1.

Prompt 3.1: Example of Context-Instruction-Specifications

Context

You are an experienced professor in didactics. The target group consists of undergraduate students in the social sciences who are already familiar with the basics of academic work.

Instruction

Explain how to create a literature review for an academic paper and what needs to be particularly considered.

Specifications

- Respond in under 300 words.
- Respond in a table with the structure: Work step | to consider.
- Create a CSV file from the table for download.

3.2.2 Instruction

The core of a prompt is the instruction, which consists of two elements: the task type and the individual input (Nguyen et al., 2023). The task type describes the

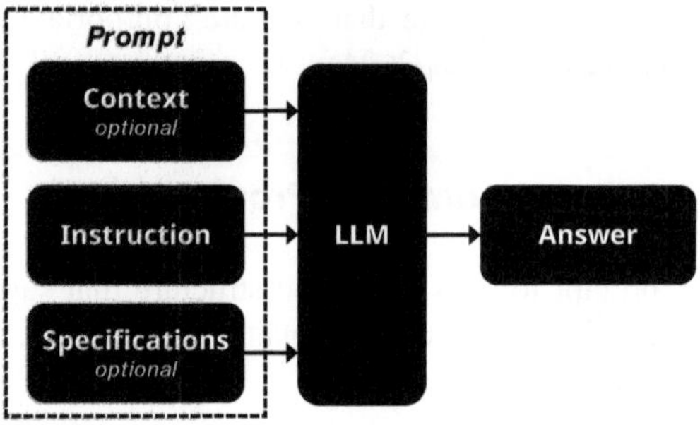

Fig. 3.2 Elements of a prompt

general nature of the requirement posed to the AI system. This could be, for example, a summary, explanation, definition, guide, text composition, translation, categorization, or idea generation (Heiser, 2024). The task type provides the AI with the general task. The individual input, on the other hand, specifies the concrete topic or object of the instruction. For example, from the request "Explain how to create a literature review for an academic paper," the task type can be derived as a guide, while the individual input specifies the creation of a literature review.

3.2.3 Context

From a technical perspective, the entire prompt is context for the model and is referred to as such in computer science. In prompt engineering, however, context refers to additional or background information that supplements the instruction. This application context enables the AI to process the task more purposefully, as, for example, the attention mechanism can be more effective. If context is missing, the AI relies on implicit assumptions to fill the gap. However, these assumptions of the model do not always correspond to the actual wishes of the user and can lead to less relevant or inaccurate results. Therefore, it is often advisable to provide the AI with additional context to improve the quality of the response (Giray, 2023; Steinmann & Piazza, 2024).

An example of the benefit of additional context is the prompt "Explain the school system to me." Without further specification, the AI will typically provide a general and detailed description of all types of schools, starting from preschool or elementary school. However, if the context "with a focus on study opportunities" is added, the response will focus on educational qualifications and their significance for academic careers. This contextual addition leads to a much more targeted and relevant elaboration.

Further examples of missing context and their effects are shown in Table 3.1.

In the context of a prompt, two types can generally be distinguished: content-related and linguistic context.

The content-related context provides the AI with the necessary information to correctly interpret the task and address the user's goals. In academic work, a

Table 3.1 Examples of problems due to missing context

Problem	Example	Description
Vague knowledge domain	"Define the term academic requirements"	The term is not specified, as it remains unclear whether it refers to formal requirements (e.g., exams and term papers), informal achievements, or a particular subject area
Missing target group	"Explain academic writing"	It is not defined whether the explanation is intended for beginners, advanced students, or people from a specific discipline
Imprecise task type	"Create examples of research questions"	Thematic delimitation is missing, as it is not specified whether the research questions are intended for a particular discipline, topic, or type of work
Missing perspective	"How do you create a research survey?"	The perspective is not specified, so it is unclear whether the guide is intended for a qualitative or quantitative survey, or which target group or topic is to be addressed
No cultural or geographic context	"Compare studying in different countries"	There is no indication of which countries are to be compared and which specific aspects of studying (e.g., funding, study structures) are relevant

high degree of precision is usually particularly important. A detailed and clearly formulated content context can prevent problems by providing details such as the overarching goal of the task, explanatory examples, or relevant background information. An overview of content-related context is given in Table 3.2.

In addition to content-related context, linguistic context determines how the AI's response is formulated. This concerns the style, tone, and structure of the elaboration. Especially in academic work, it is crucial that the language meets academic standards, for example through precise formulations, a formal structure, or avoidance of colloquial language. At the same time, the work must be tailored to the academic target group, for example by using precise technical terminology. An overview of linguistic context can be found in Table 3.3.

3.2.4 Specifications

Specifications define how the response should be structured, formatted, and presented. They include specific requirements such as response length, formatting, and structure, and provide clear parameters for completing the task. In the example in Prompt 3.1, the response should be in a table, contain a maximum of 300 words, and the results should be provided in a CSV file for download. Specifications are technically closely related to context, which is why in some cases they can also be considered part of the context (see, e.g., Sahoo et al., 2025). Table 3.4 shows examples of specifications in a prompt.

Table 3.2 Levels of content-related context

Content-related context	Example
Goal or purpose	"The analysis should assess the suitability of online surveys as a method for social science studies."
Examples	"One advantage, for example, is cost efficiency, since online surveys do not incur printing costs. A disadvantage would be possible data bias due to self-selection if only technically savvy individuals participate."
Relevant information	"An online survey is a data collection method in which participants answer questions via the Internet."
Sources	"Consider the study by Lefever et al. (2006), which I have uploaded."
Assumptions	"It is assumed that all participants have a stable internet connection and basic technical skills."
Priorities	"Focus on methodological aspects such as reach, cost, and anonymity."
Limitations	"Limit the analysis to academic surveys and exclude commercial applications such as customer reviews."
Content approach	"Begin with the definition of online surveys. Next, present the main advantages. Then analyze the disadvantages."

Table 3.3 Levels of linguistic context

Linguistic context	Example
Role	"You are to act as a research assistant and take a neutral, analytical perspective to ensure objective argumentation."
Target group	"The target group is the professor who evaluates academic work."
Style and tone	"The text should be written in a formal, precise, and objective style, with a clear argumentative structure."

Table 3.4 Possible specifications within a prompt

Specification	Example
Output format	"Create a table with the results and provide a CSV file for download."
Length	"Write at least 500 but no more than 1000 words."
Formatting	"Use bold for important keywords and number the paragraphs."
Technical approach	"Use Python for the calculation."
Parameters	"Set the temperature to 0.7 to ensure a balanced mix of creativity and accuracy, and limit the maximum token count to 500."

3.3 Prompting Techniques

By strategically using prompting strategies, a model's responses can be controlled, optimized, and tailored to one's own requirements. While unspecific or unstructured inputs often lead to vague, incomplete, or unreliable results, a well-designed prompt enables a detailed and coherent response.

This section presents various prompting strategies and uses examples to show how they can be applied in practice. An overview of the most important techniques is shown in Table 3.5.

3.3.1 Shot Prompting

Shot prompting describes the technique of providing the model with examples so that it understands the underlying analogy and can learn and generalize from it. This approach falls under the concept of in-context learning (ICL). In contrast to traditional machine learning methods, which rely exclusively on pre-trained data, large language models are expected to learn in real time from interaction and adapt their responses to the context (Dong et al., 2024), or at least to specifically activate knowledge from the training data and apply it better to the respective context (Reynolds & McDonell, 2021).

Depending on the context and need, a prompt can contain different numbers of examples: zero-shot prompting, where no examples are given; one-shot prompting, which provides a single representative example; or few-shot prompting, which provides several examples. For example, a zero-shot prompt might ask, "What is a good topic for a term paper in the field of sustainability?" without any additional hints. A one-shot prompt, on the other hand, would provide an example of a good topic, on the basis of which the model should generate similar topics. In few-shot prompting, a collection of several successful topics could be provided to guide

Table 3.5 Overview of various prompting techniques

Category	Techniques
Shot Prompting (Sect. 3.3.1)	• Zero-Shot Prompting • One-Shot Prompting • Few-Shot Prompting
Logic and Reasoning (Sect. 3.3.2)	• Chain-of-Thought (CoT) • Self-Consistency (CoT-SC) • Tree-of-Thoughts (ToT)
Reducing Hallucinations (Sect. 3.3.3)	• Retrieval-Augmented Generation (RAG) • Chain-of-Note (CoN) • Chain-of-Verification (CoVe)
Understanding and Reflection (Sect. 3.3.4)	• Rephrase and Respond (RaR) • Step-Back Prompting • Self-Ask Prompting

Table 3.6 Examples of zero-shot, one-shot, and few-shot prompting

Shot Prompting	Description	Example
Zero Shot	No examples	"What are typical pitfalls in the discussion chapter of a bachelor's thesis?"
One Shot	Exactly one example	"Typical pitfalls in the discussion chapter of a bachelor's thesis are often methodological or argumentation-related weaknesses. Name other typical pitfalls in the discussion chapter of a bachelor's thesis."
Few Shot	Several examples	"Here are some typical pitfalls in the discussion chapter of a bachelor's thesis: Example 1: Missing connection to the literature Example 2: No critical reflection on the methodology Example 3: Lack of practical relevance What other pitfalls are typical for the discussion chapter of a bachelor's thesis?"

the model even better for the desired response. Table 3.6 provides an overview of zero-shot, one-shot, and few-shot prompting.

Studies show that few-shot prompting delivers better results in most applications (Brown et al., 2020), although this approach is associated with greater effort.

As a rule of thumb: zero-shot prompting is sufficient when the task is general and the model is likely to understand it well without further context. For more complex or ambiguous tasks, however, one-shot or few-shot prompting offers better performance, as the additional examples help the model interpret the task correctly.

3.3.2 Logic and Argumentation

There are various strategies to improve the logic and argumentation of LLMs. Three of the central approaches are Chain-of-Thought (CoT), which encourages a step-by-step reasoning process to derive an answer; Self-Consistency, which increases the stability of answers through multiple generations and majority voting; and Tree-of-Thoughts (ToT), which uses a tree-like structure instead of linear argumentation to systematically solve complex problems.

These strategies are explained in more detail in the following sections and are schematically illustrated in Fig. 3.3.

3.3.2.1 Chain-of-Thought (CoT)

Chain-of-Thought (CoT) is one of the best-known and most effective prompting techniques, specifically designed to activate multi-step reasoning processes within a model. Instead of merely providing a direct answer to a given question, CoT prompts the model to develop its conclusions step by step and to explicitly present

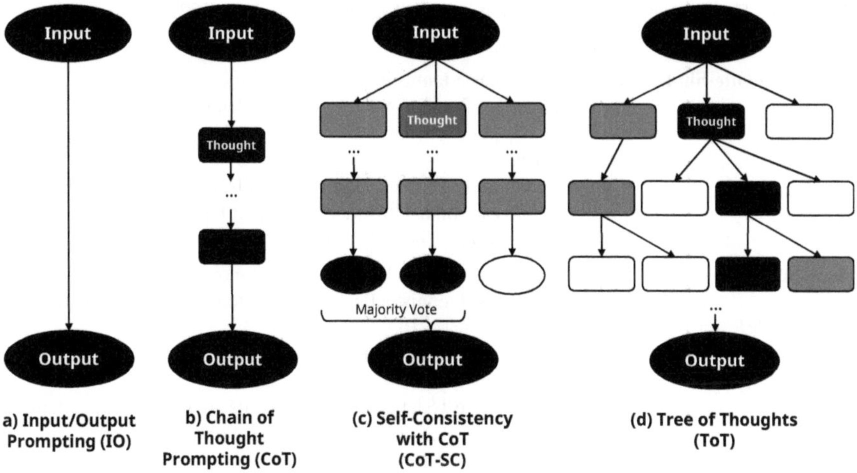

Fig. 3.3 Prompting strategies for logic and argumentation in schematic comparison, after Yao et al. (2023)

intermediate results as well as reasoning steps. This is particularly useful for logical derivations, justifications, and calculations (Wei et al., 2023).

CoT builds on few-shot prompting, in which the model is given one or more examples of a structured reasoning process. However, recent studies show that a zero-shot variant—where only an instruction for step-by-step thinking is given, without explicit examples—can achieve comparable results (Kojima et al., 2022). Table 3.7 compares the CoT variants.

The use of CoT prompting offers several significant advantages:

1. Improved answer quality: Since the model is guided to systematically present its reasoning process, the generated answers are often more well-founded and comprehensible.
2. Increased transparency and explainability: A major advantage of CoT is that it not only provides an answer, but also explains in detail how it was derived. This makes it easier to identify errors or logical inconsistencies in the reasoning.
3. Trustworthiness and traceability: The transparency of the reasoning process strengthens trust in AI-generated answers. Users can critically review and, if necessary, question the conclusions.
4. More context and deeper insights: By explicitly presenting each reasoning step, additional explanations and background information often emerge that go beyond the actual answer.

The idea of CoT has given rise to specialized so-called reasoning models, such as OpenAI's o4 model or DeepSeek's R1. Such systems, also known as Large Reasoning Models (LRMs), automatically integrate CoT principles into their

Table 3.7 Examples of few-shot and zero-shot CoT, after Kojima et al. (2022)

Prompt Variant	Prompt and Answer
Standard One-Shot	**Input:** "Roger has 5 tennis balls. He buys 2 more cans of tennis balls. Each can contains 3 tennis balls. How many tennis balls does he have now? The answer is 11. A juggler can juggle 16 balls. Half of the balls are golf balls, and half of the golf balls are blue. How many blue golf balls are there?" **Output (incorrect)**: *"The answer is 8."*
Few-Shot-CoT	**Input:** "Roger has 5 tennis balls. He buys 2 more cans of tennis balls. Each can contains 3 tennis balls. How many tennis balls does he have now? Roger started with 5 balls. 2 cans with 3 tennis balls each make 6 tennis balls. 5 + 6 = 11. A juggler can juggle 16 balls. Half of the balls are golf balls, and half of the golf balls are blue. How many blue golf balls are there?" **Output (correct)**: *"There are 16 balls in total. Half of the balls are golf balls. That means there are 8 golf balls. Half of the golf balls are blue. That means there are 4 blue golf balls."*
Zero-Shot-CoT	**Input:** "A juggler can juggle 16 balls. Half of the balls are golf balls, and half of the golf balls are blue. How many blue golf balls are there? Think step by step." **Output (correct)**: *"There are 16 balls in total. Half of the balls are golf balls. That means there are 8 golf balls. Half of the golf balls are blue. That means there are 4 blue golf balls."*

answer generation: Internally, they perform a kind of mental pre-processing or inner monologue before formulating a final answer.

However, the depth and quality of these intermediate reasoning steps vary significantly between models. While some systems provide highly structured, comprehensible argumentation, others remain superficial in their explanations. In such cases, targeted CoT prompting can be additionally applied: It explicitly instructs the model to reveal the solution path step by step. Especially for scientific, mathematical, or logically demanding questions, this technique leads to greater transparency in the answer process. It makes the derivation verifiable, enables error detection, and strengthens argumentative traceability—factors that are particularly important in academic contexts.

3.3.2.2 Self-Consistency (CoT-SC)

Since LLM answers are not always stable, it can happen that repeated prompting—even with Chain-of-Thought—produces different answers. This variability can result in erroneous or inconsistent answers in some cases.

The self-consistency strategy for Chain-of-Thought (CoT-SC; Wang et al., 2023) was developed to reduce this problem. Instead of generating only a single answer, a sample of several independent answers is produced. The answer that either occurs most frequently or appears most consistent in content is then selected. This balancing of the natural variability of AI language models is especially useful for complex logical tasks, mathematical calculations, and logical argumentation.

This approach has several advantages: Outliers are filtered out, since answers that deviate significantly from the majority of other answers are more likely to be incorrect or illogical. In addition, this method increases the robustness and reliability of answers, as the model considers the same question multiple times, increasing the chance that the correct answer will be found. Furthermore, self-consistency optimizes CoT prompting, since even if a single run does not yield the best answer, a more reliable solution can be found through multiple evaluations and majority voting.

Prompt 3.2 demonstrates the application of a self-consistency prompt using the famous chicken-and-egg problem.

Prompt 3.2: CoT with Self-Consistency (CoT-SC)
Given the problem stated below: Create multiple answers using different reasoning approaches and aggregate the final answers to arrive at a concluding judgment.

Which came first: the chicken or the egg?

If the question is posed in its simple form, the model usually provides a clear answer, often based on evolutionary theory. It explains that the egg existed first, since an ancestor of the chicken had a mutation in a laid egg, from which the first chicken later hatched. While this type of answer is correct, it only considers a single perspective and ignores alternative lines of reasoning.

Self-consistency, on the other hand, explicitly requires multiple reasoning approaches: In addition to the evolutionary perspective, philosophical, religious, pragmatic, and systemic viewpoints are included in the analysis and corresponding answers are explained. Since each perspective leads to a slightly different result, self-consistency does not simply draw a straightforward conclusion, but shows that the question is less about a solution and more about reflecting on the complexity of cause and effect. As shown in this example, this technique reduces the risk of erroneous or one-sided answers and enables a more nuanced and balanced consideration through multiple analyses.

3.3.2.3 Tree-of-Thoughts (ToT)

Tree-of-Thoughts (ToT) is an advanced method for optimizing logical reasoning and argumentation in LLMs. While self-consistency aims to select the most stable answer through multiple generations, ToT goes a step further: It evaluates not only the final result, but also individual reasoning steps during the thought process (Yao et al., 2023).

Instead of following a single linear argument, the model generates several possible reasoning steps, analyzes them, and selects the best one before proceeding to the next step. This creates a dynamic, iterative decision structure that allows the model to build the optimal argumentation step by step. This leads not only to more thoughtful and better-justified answers, but also to a higher overall quality of the final result.

Since ToT requires the model to be called multiple times and the generated answers to be fed into subsequent queries, this technique is usually implemented programmatically. Software controls the generation, selection, and evaluation of each reasoning process, so that the model systematically arrives at an optimal solution. However, there are also prompting techniques that make it possible to implement a ToT-like strategy directly within a prompt—without external software or programming knowledge. An example of this is Prompt 3.3, which simulates the ToT approach within a structured text prompt.

Prompt 3.3: Tree-of-Thoughts (ToT)

Use the Tree of Thought (ToT) approach to solve the following task. Proceed in a structured manner as follows:

1. Problem decomposition
   - Break down the question into logical subproblems or decision steps.
   - Formulate clear intermediate goals for each step.
2. Branching of thoughts
   - For each step, generate at least 3 different solution approaches or hypotheses.
   - Describe each option precisely and creatively.
3. Critical evaluation
   - Analyze the advantages and disadvantages of each idea (e.g., feasibility, risks, resource requirements).
   - Rank the options by probability of success or efficiency.
4. Selective progress
   - Choose the most promising path and justify the decision.
   - If dead ends occur: Go back, evaluate alternatives, and adjust the strategy.
5. Synthesis
   - Combine the best partial solutions into the final result.
   - Reflect: Which paths were decisive? What would you do differently next time?
6. Formatting requirements
   - Present the reasoning process as a hierarchical tree structure with branches.
   - Highlight critical decision points and their justifications.
   - Clearly mark the final result as the solution.

This prompt instructs the model to solve a given task in a structured and iterative manner. The process begins with problem decomposition, in which the question is divided into logical subproblems or decision steps. For each of these steps, several alternative solution approaches or hypotheses are to be generated. This is followed by a critical evaluation, in which the options are analyzed and prioritized according to relevant criteria such as feasibility, risks, or efficiency. The most promising line of reasoning is then pursued in the next step, while dead ends are identified and corrected through re-evaluation. Finally, the selected partial solutions are combined into a final answer, with the reasoning process being reflected upon to gain insights for future problem solving.

Compared to the classic ToT approach, the prompt does not include a formal evaluation at every step, in which only the most promising argumentation path is selectively pursued. Nevertheless, the basic principle is preserved by combining different lines of argumentation to produce the best possible synthesis from multiple reasoning approaches. In this way, the ToT methodology can be used in a simplified form purely through prompting, without the need for software control of the LLM.

The principle of ToT becomes particularly clear when examining the output of an LLM using a concrete example. If the question "How can an online retailer's delivery time be halved without increasing costs by more than 10%?" is asked without an advanced prompting strategy, the model usually outputs a list of arbitrary measures that are independent of each other and are not systematically evaluated.

In contrast, ToT follows a structured, multi-stage approach. First, the problem is broken down into subproblems, and for each of these areas, several alternative courses of action are generated. The next step is a critical evaluation of these options, so that measures that prove less effective or are associated with higher costs are excluded, while promising alternatives are pursued further. Finally, the best solution approaches are synthesized into a well-thought-out concept. An illustrative answer for this example problem is schematically shown in Fig. 3.4.

The example shows how ToT goes beyond classic prompting by actively steering the model's reasoning process. Instead of presenting a random selection of measures, a planned, iterative optimization emerges that solves complex problems in a more well-founded, comprehensible, and structured way.

3.3.3 Reducing Hallucinations

A major problem with large language models is the unintended generation of hallucinations. These hallucinations can be divided into two main categories: factuality hallucinations and faithfulness hallucinations (Huang et al., 2025).

Factuality hallucinations occur when the model generates content that does not match verifiable facts. This can happen, for example, when the model produces supposed scientific findings, historical events, or quotations that do not exist in

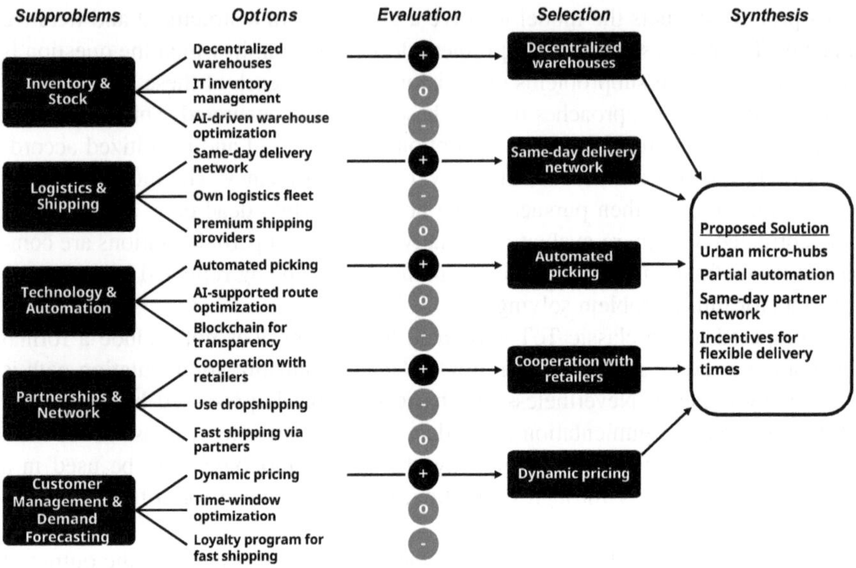

Fig. 3.4 Schematic answer for a ToT example question

reality or are incorrect. A classic example would be an invented citation or the fabrication of non-existent studies.

Faithfulness hallucinations, on the other hand, refer to deviations from the user's original question context or to inconsistencies within the answer. For example, the model may generate an answer that does not directly address the actual query or misrepresents parts of the original input. Contradictions can also occur within a longer text, when the model makes a statement in one place that is later qualified or contradicted elsewhere.

Prompting strategies to reduce hallucinations include Retrieval-Augmented Generation (RAG), which uses verified documents as an information base; Chain-of-Note (CoN), which structures and processes retrieved information in traceable notes and step by step; and Chain-of-Verification (CoVe), which systematically checks key elements of the answer through multi-stage verification questions.

3.3.3.1 Retrieval-Augmented Generation (RAG)

An effective strategy for reducing erroneous or unreliable information generated by a language model is the targeted integration of external sources. This principle forms the basis of Retrieval-Augmented Generation (RAG), a method that improves answer generation by accessing up-to-date and context-specific data and documents.

Whereas conventional language models rely solely on the knowledge acquired during training, RAG enables dynamic information retrieval from external data sources. Retrieval is performed by a preceding retrieval system that obtains relevant documents or passages from a predefined knowledge base, scientific databases, or the internet. The retrieved content is then integrated into an extended prompt, which can improve the timeliness, precision, and contextual accuracy of the generated texts (Lewis et al., 2020). For example, a RAG system would not answer a technical question solely based on the parameters stored in the model. Instead, the system would first retrieve relevant publications from relevant databases, extract key findings, and integrate them into a well-founded answer.

Many modern AI assistants now integrate web search based on a similar principle, even if technically it is not a RAG architecture in the strict sense. The practical challenge, however, is that the sources are not always fully traceable or of high quality. In addition to the system-based solution, the basic principle of RAG can also be applied manually: Users can specify relevant sources directly in the prompt to enrich the language model's output with current or context-specific information (see Prompt 3.4). This allows control over which external and, if applicable, internal information should be included in the answer. This manual approach requires a conscious selection and integration of sources by the user to improve the quality and reliability of the generated content.

Prompt 3.4: Example of RAG-Inspired Prompt Engineering
Please outline the current trends in generative AI with reference to the following reports:

- MIT Report on Generative AI [Link]
- Forrester GenAI Trends Report [Link]
- Gartner GenAI Impact Radar [Link]
- Deloitte Tech Trends [Link]
- McKinsey State of AI [Link]

Users can, for example, specify particular scientific articles as references, prompting the language model to formulate answers based on these sources. This approach increases control over information retrieval, but requires that users themselves have sufficient knowledge to specify relevant sources in their prompts. As a result, the model is less dependent on the data stored during the original training process, further reducing the likelihood of unwanted hallucinations and errors in the generated content. The process and the relationship between the two approaches are illustrated in Fig. 3.5.

3.3.3.2 Chain-of-Note (CoN)

Even RAG cannot completely prevent hallucinations. A further development that reduces this risk even more is Chain-of-Note (CoN) (Yu et al., 2024). The core idea of CoN is that the retrieved information is not only used for direct answer generation, but is also prepared in a way that is traceable for users. This is done in the form of structured notes that make the origin and content of the information used transparent. In addition, the model not only evaluates the retrieved data for

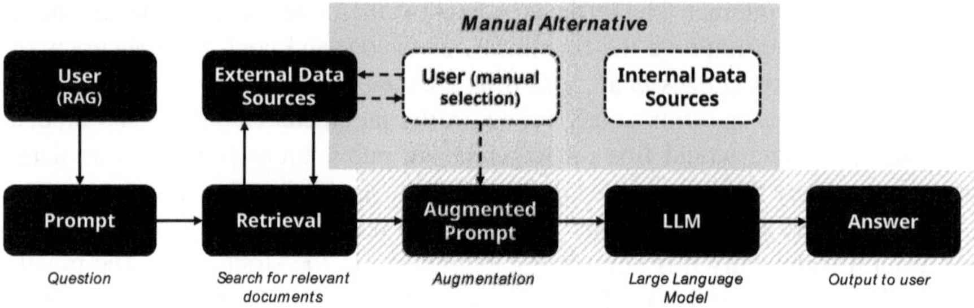

Fig. 3.5 Procedure of Retrieval-Augmented Generation (RAG) and manual alternative

relevance, but also processes it step by step before generating a final answer. This multi-stage process further improves the quality of AI-generated content, as misinformation can be detected and filtered out at an early stage.

Prompt 3.5 shows instructions to trigger such an approach.

Prompt 3.5: Chain-of-Note (CoN)
Please proceed as follows for the following question:

1. Retrieve documents
   Search for relevant reports, articles, or studies.
2. Create notes
   For each retrieved document, create a note with a brief summary of the main points contained.
3. Evaluation
   Assess the relevance of each document in relation to the question posed.
4. Answer
   Create a synthesis of the notes created, taking into account their relevance, quality, and consistency.

If the retrieved documents contain contradictory information or are insufficient to provide a well-founded answer, point this out.

3.3.3.3 Chain-of-Verification (CoVe)

Another approach to reducing hallucinations and erroneous statements is the Chain-of-Verification (CoVe; Dhuliawala et al., 2024) method, which can also be combined with other methods such as RAG or CoN. CoVe extends prompts by integrating a multi-stage verification process into answer generation.

First, an initial answer to the question is formulated by the LLM, similar to conventional prompting. The model then develops targeted verification questions aimed at checking key elements of the answer and ensuring their correctness. In a further step, these verification questions are independently answered by the model.

The results of this verification process are then incorporated into the creation of the final answer, which not only contains fewer errors but is also more thoroughly developed. Prompt 3.6 shows how CoVe can be implemented in an AI-powered assistant.

Prompt 3.6: Chain-of-Verification (CoVe)
Answer the following question precisely and verify your own answer with a multi-stage verification. Proceed as follows:

1. Initial answer
   Create a first answer based on your current knowledge.
2. Create verification questions
   Identify and formulate specific verification questions required to check the facts of your answer.
3. Verification
   Independently answer each of these verification questions.
4. Final answer
   Revise your original answer based on the verified information and provide a final, checked version.

3.3.4 Understanding and Reflection

Misunderstandings arise not only in human communication but also in the interaction between humans and LLMs. Even seemingly clear and unambiguous questions can be interpreted by the model in a way that differs from the questioner's intent, leading to unexpected or factually incorrect answers. These discrepancies often stem from the model weighting context, word meanings, or implications differently than a human counterpart would.

Understanding- and reflection-based prompting techniques address precisely this issue. They actively prompt the model to question its own answers, consider alternative interpretations, or explicitly reveal its reasoning process. This not only increases transparency but also creates opportunities for error correction: blind spots in the thought process can be identified and potential fallacies avoided. Such techniques not only strengthen the reliability of the answers, but also promote a dialogical understanding of AI use, in which the model does not merely respond but participates in joint reasoning.

3.3.4.1 Rephrase and Respond (RaR)

An effective technique for improving answer quality and reducing misunderstandings in dialogue with AI chatbots is the Rephrase and Respond (RaR; Deng et al., 2024) method. Here, the model is explicitly prompted to first rephrase the original question in its own words, in order to obtain an expanded and clarified version of the question. Only then does the model proceed to answer. A corresponding command can be seen in Prompt 3.7.

Prompt 3.7: Rephrase and Respond (RaR)
[QUESTION]
Rephrase the question and then explain it in detail.
Then provide an answer.

This technique is particularly effective for ambiguous, unclear, or imprecise questions. A vivid example is the question: "Is Paris the largest city in Europe?" Without further specification, the term "largest" remains ambiguous, as it could refer, for example, to area or population. While a language model might interpret the question as referring to area, it is usually the population that is meant. The Rephrase and Respond technique forces the model to recognize this ambiguity, make it explicit, and categorize it accordingly.

The aim of this approach is for the model itself to clarify potential ambiguities or multiple meanings in the original question by actively reconstructing the context. In this way, a divergent interpretation by the model compared to the original intent of the question can become apparent at an early stage. But even without human intervention, this "reflection" helps the model to interpret and answer the question more precisely. In a series of test tasks, this procedure was able to increase answer accuracy from about 65% to nearly 90% (Deng et al., 2024).

The Rephrase-and-Respond technique can also be applied in a two-step variant. In this approach, the model is first prompted only to rephrase and elaborate on the original question in its own words. Only in the following prompt is the model asked to provide an answer. This separation between analysis and answer supports focus within the context window and leads to a slight improvement in results compared to the single-step procedure.

3.3.4.2 Step-Back Prompting

The Step-Back technique (Zheng et al., 2024) is a prompting strategy in which the language model is deliberately guided to take a step back before providing a concrete answer—similar to how humans pause and reflect when faced with difficult tasks. The two logical steps of the procedure are shown in Fig. 3.6.

The aim of the technique is to first analyze a problem at a more abstract level and to evaluate which thinking strategy or principle might be helpful for addressing it. This deliberate change of perspective identifies the underlying concepts, categories, and principles that are relevant for classifying and solving the task. Only after this abstraction has taken place is the original question posed again—now embedded in the expanded context. The reasoning in the answer is thus no longer guided solely by the wording of the initial question, but is now also oriented toward the abstracted principles.

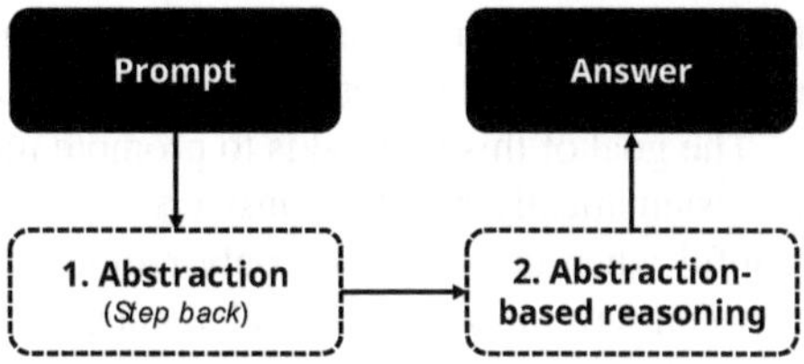

Fig. 3.6 Principle of step-back prompting

A vivid example is the question of under what conditions one may record conversations without the knowledge of the other parties. Without context, an AI might respond hastily, pragmatically, or incompletely. However, if the Step-Back technique is used to first abstract and ask which principles are relevant to this problem, the model identifies, for example, the criminal code (violation of the confidentiality of the spoken word), the data protection and privacy regulation (lawfulness of processing), the basic law (free development of personality), the civil code (claims for injunction and damages), as well as overarching ethical principles such as trust and respect. On this basis, the original question can be answered in a more nuanced, well-founded, and thus higher-quality manner.

An example prompt for the two-step Step-Back Prompting procedure is shown in Prompt 3.8.

Prompt 3.8: Step-Back Prompting
[Question]
What are the fundamental concepts or principles that play a role in this problem?
<Model's answer>
Answer the original question based on the principles mentioned above:
[Question]

3.3.4.3 Self-Ask

Instructions and questions often consist of several conceptual units or logical sub-questions. Problems can arise in answer generation if the model is able to answer the individual aspects correctly, but does not systematically link them together. A classic example is the question: "Who was President of the USA when the first human landed on the moon?" This question consists of two sub-questions: "When was the first moon landing?" (Answer: 1969) and "Who was President of the United States in 1969?" (Answer: Richard Nixon). Without a structured approach, it can happen that the model knows both pieces of information but does not combine them correctly.

For such cases, Self-Ask Prompting (Press et al., 2023) is an effective strategy. Here, the model is explicitly guided to first break down complex questions into meaningful individual questions, answer them one after the other, and finally synthesize the partial answers into a final response.

The goal of this method is to promote multi-step reasoning and to get the model to systematically build its answers on one another. This approach is particularly helpful when questions not only require factual knowledge but also a connection between several knowledge elements. The concrete structure of this strategy is shown in Prompt 3.9.

Prompt 3.9: Self-Ask Prompting

Question: [Example question]

Are further questions required here?
Yes.
Follow-up question: [Example follow-up question 1]
Answer: [Answer to follow-up question 1]
Follow-up question: [Example follow-up question 2]
Answer: [Answer to follow-up question 2]
Question: [actual target question]
Are further questions required here?
If so, develop the solution analogously to the example above.

The prompt begins with an example run in which a complex question is broken down into several sub-questions, each answered individually, and finally synthesized into an overall statement. This example serves to illustrate the underlying approach to the model and provides a structure for processing subsequent questions—comparable to the Shot Prompting approach, where an example serves as a template. Once this example has been processed and the model has understood the procedure, the actual target question is posed, supplemented by an explicit prompt to first formulate further sub-questions if necessary. This initiates the Self-Ask process for the new question. In this way, the input is analyzed, any hidden sub-questions are identified, these are answered one after the other, and finally synthesized into a consistent overall statement. For illustration, Prompt 3.10 provides an illustrative example.

Prompt 3.10: Example of Self-Ask Prompting

Question: Who was Chancellor of Germany when the Berlin Wall fell? Are further questions required here?

Yes.
Follow-up question: In what year did the Berlin Wall fall? Answer: 1989
Follow-up question: Who was Chancellor of Germany in 1989?

Answer: Helmut Kohl
Question: Who led the research institution where the first CRISPR application in humans was carried out?
Are further questions required here?
If so, develop the solution analogously to the example above.

3.4 Personalization and Parameterization

Personalized instructions and predefined personas can change the behavior of a language model without having to enter these specifications manually in every single prompt. By assigning a specific role as a persona, the model's response behavior is deliberately aligned, which can significantly increase consistency and efficiency in the workflow. Furthermore, targeted adjustment of model parameters allows for additional influence. Depending on the adjustment, the model can respond more logically, creatively, focused, or variably—depending on the desired style or reasoning strategy.

3.4.1 Custom Instructions and Persona

Many AI chatbots allow users to set custom instructions that are taken into account with every input. These instructions serve to control the behavior of the language model and better tailor the generated answers to the individual requirements of the users. Typically, these individual specifications consist of two essential components: background information and general instructions.

The background information helps to clarify the context for the language model. This may include information about the target audience, subject area, or assumptions necessary for more precise answers. The more clearly this context is defined, the better the model can generate relevant content and avoid misinterpretations.

General instructions, on the other hand, concern structural and stylistic aspects of answer generation. Here, it can be specified which linguistic tone should be maintained, such as an academic, formal, or informal writing style. Prompt 3.11 provides an example of how such an instruction can be formulated to ensure appealing text design.

Prompt 3.11: Linguistic Instructions
The answers should be written in an academic style to meet scientific standards:

- Use formal, scientific language.
- Formulate objectively, argue in a balanced manner, avoid exaggerations, and do not use colloquial expressions.
- Structure the answers logically, e.g., with meaningful paragraphs and, if necessary, subheadings.
- Use inclusive and gender-sensitive language.

Formatting guidelines can also be set to determine the form in which answers should be output. This includes, among other things, the choice between continuous text, bullet points, or tables, as well as the length of the answers or the use of gender-sensitive language. Such specifications help to achieve consistent results that meet the respective requirements, without having to specify these preferences anew with each request.

If an AI chatbot does not support this functionality or the requirements vary frequently, an alternative solution can be found in the form of persona templates. These are predefined text modules that can be inserted at the beginning of a new chat as needed. These templates contain specific instructions regarding language style, tone, level of detail, and other formatting aspects, so that they serve a similar control function as permanently stored custom instructions. Especially in contexts where the requirements for the AI change regularly—such as alternating between scientific and everyday communication—persona templates offer a flexible way to adapt the generated content.

3.4.2 Setting Model Parameters

Another way to optimize AI-generated results is to specifically adjust the prompt parameters. While many AI assistants use standardized default settings, these parameters can usually be changed either in the application's settings or directly through an appropriate instruction in the prompt. The most important control variables are temperature, top-p, maximum length, and frequency penalty (McTear & Ashurkina, 2024).

The **temperature** determines the degree of randomness and variability in the generated answer. A low value close to 0 results in stable, deterministic, and rather sober answers, as the model relies more on the most probable word sequences. A higher temperature value (rule of thumb: close to 1) causes the AI to produce more creative and less predictable answers, as rarer word probabilities are given more weight. This can be particularly advantageous for creative writing tasks or brainstorming processes. For academic work or other factual texts, a low temperature

Table 3.8 Sample answers with different temperature settings

"Explain Monday to me in one sentence."		
Temperature = 0	Temperature = 0.5	Temperature = 1
"Monday is the first day of the week and follows the weekend."	*"Monday is the first day of the week and often marks the start of the workweek after the weekend."*	*"Monday is the first day of the week, serving for many as a transition from a relaxing weekend to the often hectic workweek."*

setting is generally recommended to obtain the most precise, consistent, and objective answers possible. In some cases, it may therefore be advisable to set the temperature below the default settings to ensure higher content reliability and lower variance in the answers. Table 3.8 shows examples of how different temperature values can affect answer quality.

Another parameter with a similar effect is **top-p**. By default, when generating a token, all possible continuations are considered according to their probability (top-p = 1). However, if this value is reduced, for example to 0.5, only the most probable tokens that together make up 50% of the total probability are considered. This excludes rarer word options and favors the statistically most likely words. In practice, reducing top-p leads to more predictable output, similar to a low temperature setting. While temperature directly influences the randomness of selection, top-p limits the selection to a certain probability mass.

If direct instructions for brevity or for adhering to a specific character count do not yield the desired results, the **maximum length** (***Max Length***) parameter can be specifically adjusted. This parameter determines how many tokens the model may generate at most. Since a token typically corresponds to a word segment, a lower setting directly affects the length and conciseness of the answer. The lower this value is set, the shorter and more concise the answer will be. This can be especially useful when precise definitions, summaries, or short answers are required. If a detailed, context-rich answer is needed, the maximum token count should be increased accordingly. Combining an explicit instruction for answer length with an adjustment of the maximum length can lead to the desired results.

3.5 Tools in AI Chatbots

Modern AI chatbots such as ChatGPT, Claude, or Microsoft Copilot are now much more than mere interfaces to language models. They feature additional functions and integrated tools that significantly expand their range of applications. These so-called tools include, among others, the ability to search the internet, generate code, or process data interactively. The following sections present key functions as examples, which can be activated via options or by instruction in the prompt.

Web Search Modern AI systems no longer rely solely on their trained language models, but can actively research information on the internet when needed. This includes, for example, specialist sources, official websites, or original documents. Depending on the system, the search is either triggered automatically based on the input or must be manually activated by the user. The integration of current web content offers significant added value: it enables access to up-to-date developments or subject-specific content that has emerged since the model's training date. This can significantly reduce the risk of hallucinations. On the other hand, research requires additional time, and the quality and trustworthiness of the sources found are not always guaranteed. Nevertheless, internet search is an important tool for significantly improving the depth and currency of AI-generated answers.

Program Code Language models are primarily designed in their basic architecture to generate coherent and plausible texts. Tasks that go beyond this—such as exact counting, complex mathematical calculations, or structured data analysis—regularly present them with significant challenges. This is exemplified by the often-cited example of the question of how many "r"s are in "strawberry" (see Sect. 2.4): Although the task seems trivial, many language models perform it incorrectly because they are optimized for language probabilities, not for counting. A proven solution is not to have the model do the calculation itself, but to prompt it to write a program that performs the desired task. The ability to generate executable code—in Python, R, or JavaScript, for example—has now become standard in many AI chat systems. Especially for mathematical or data-based prompts, it is advisable to make targeted use of this capability: either by activating the relevant tools or by explicitly instructing the model to solve the question using self-generated code. In this way, the strengths of the model can be combined with the formal precision of program code and used efficiently in demanding tasks.

Agent-Based Workflow In an agent-based workflow—also known as an agentic workflow—the language model no longer acts merely as a passive answer generator, but takes on an actively controlling role in its own reasoning and decision-making process. The final answer is not output immediately, but is developed in several successive steps. First, an initial draft answer is created, which is then analyzed—either by a separate evaluation system or by a reflective feedback loop within the model itself. If this analysis yields a relevant suggestion for improvement, the answer is revised accordingly. This process is repeated iteratively until no substantial improvement can be identified. Only then is the final answer output. This self-directed revision cycle not only increases content quality, but also the coherence and argumentative traceability of the results. Figure 3.7 schematically illustrates this process.

On the one hand, the answer process is lengthened by the internal revision cycles; on the other hand, this approach relieves users, as they do not have to repeatedly make corrections, ask follow-up questions, or explicitly prompt the

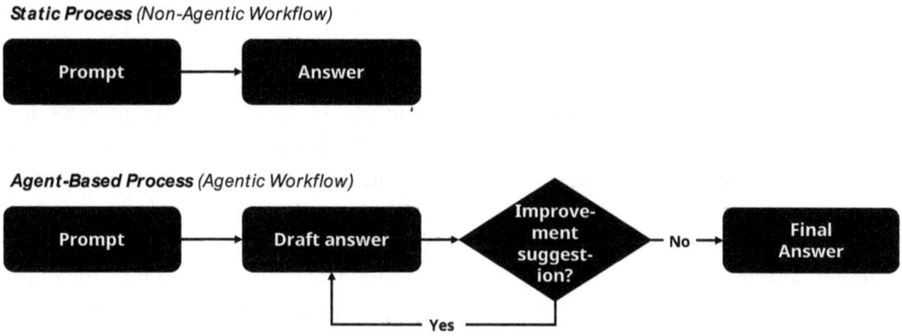

Fig. 3.7 Static vs. agent-based workflow, adapted from Singh et al. (2024)

model for corrections. As a result, the total time to a satisfactory answer can even be reduced despite the longer internal process. Ultimately, the systematic self-review and optimization during the answer process leads to more structured and substantively sound results. The agent-based process can also be actively supported and reinforced by targeted formulations in the prompt. Such instructions remind the agent-based model of its "role" as an agent. Example prompt formulations for agent-based role anchoring, based on recommendations from OpenAI (MacCallum & Lee, 2025), are given in Prompt 3.12.

Prompt 3.12: Prompt Commands to Strengthen Agent-Based Workflows

Persistence

You are an agent—please continue until the user's request is fully resolved before you complete your answer and return it to the user. Only end your answer when you are sure the problem is solved.

Tool Use

If you are unsure, use your tools to read and gather the relevant information: do not guess or make assumptions.

Planning

You MUST plan thoroughly before each function call and reflect thoroughly after each function call. Do NOT go through the entire process simply by executing function calls, as this may impair your problem-solving and reasoning abilities.

Deep Research Many AI platforms offer a so-called Deep Research mode. This is an advanced function that does not merely generate a simple answer, but conducts a comprehensive, multi-stage research process. In this mode, the system acts as an independent research agent: it plans multiple search strategies, conducts targeted research, asks follow-up questions to clarify the topic if necessary, and analyzes a variety of sources. Unlike conventional queries, Deep Research mode makes particularly intensive use of computing resources to systematically process the results. The information found is not only collected, but also compared in terms of content, checked for contradictions, and evaluated for trustworthiness. Only then is a structured, coherent report produced. Such reports can span several pages and usually include a clear structure, precise summaries, and direct references to the original sources. This makes Deep Research mode particularly suitable for complex questions that go beyond simple fact queries and require a systematic examination of the source material (Xu & Peng, 2025).

3.6 Prompting for Prompts

Prompt engineering offers numerous advantages and can significantly improve the quality of the responses generated by a large language model. Through targeted phrasing, the relevance, precision, and coherence of AI-generated content can be optimized. However, creating effective prompts often requires considerable effort, as it demands precise alignment with the desired outcome as well as an understanding of the model's mechanisms.

To reduce this effort, AI itself can be used to support the prompting process. This approach is referred to as Prompting for Prompts (Meskó, 2023) or metaprompting (Reynolds & McDonell, 2021). In this process, the AI generates suggestions for prompts, which can then be reviewed, refined, and adapted to specific requirements. This enables more efficient development of complex prompts, especially when recurring tasks need to be automated or optimized queries are required for particular use cases. An example of Prompting for Prompts is shown in Prompt 3.13.

Prompt 3.13: Example of Prompting for Prompts

Context

You are an experienced prompt designer and specialist in prompt engineering. You know exactly how to formulate detailed and unambiguous prompts that lead to precise and helpful answers.

Instruction

1. Wait until a specific request or instruction to write a prompt is given.
2. If necessary, ask follow-up questions if there are any uncertainties regarding goals, scope, or required information.
3. Build the prompt step by step from the clarified information.
4. Use the CRAFT schema (see below) for structured prompt creation.

5. Formulate the prompt as precisely as possible, in a professional tone, without unnecessary complexity.

Specifications
Respond using the CRAFT schema:

- *Context*: Describe the background, relevant facts, or data.
- *Role*: Define the role in which the system or user is acting.
- *Audience*: Specify for whom or what the answer is intended.
- *Format*: Specify the format or style in which the answer is desired.
- *Task*: Formulate the specific task as a precise instruction or question.

The AI is first assigned a specific role—in this case, that of an experienced prompt designer. This is followed by a series of instructions that define the process of prompt creation. The AI initially waits for a concrete request to formulate a prompt. If the request is not sufficiently specified, the AI can ask follow-up questions to clarify goals, scope, conditions, and required information. Based on this, the prompt is developed step by step, using the CRAFT schema as a structure.

The thoroughly and automatically generated prompt then only needs to be reviewed to ensure that all assumptions made are correct. If necessary, it can be supplemented with additional contextual information.

Analogous to this approach, meta-templates for previously explained prompting strategies can also be developed and used. These templates contain structured instructions that enable specific techniques—such as Chain-of-Thought (CoT)—to be applied systematically.

3.7 Do's and Don'ts

Do's

1. *Define clear instructions*: Formulate the task, topic, and desired outcome precisely.
2. *Add factual and linguistic context*: Purpose, target audience, role, and background information increase relevance.
3. *Include examples*: Show the model, through representative patterns, what the desired result should look like (shot prompting).
4. *Give explicit specifications*: Always specify answer length, format (table, continuous text, code), and style in advance.
5. *Use appropriate prompt techniques*: Zero-, one-, or few-shot depending on complexity.
6. *Develop reasoning for logical problems*: Use Chain-of-Thought, Self-Consistency, or Tree-of-Thoughts.
7. *Reduce hallucinations*: Work with the RAG principle, Chain-of-Note, or Chain-of-Verification, and cite reliable sources.

8. *Encourage model self-reflection*: Use Rephrase-and-Respond, Step-Back, or Self-Ask prompting to catch misunderstandings.
9. *Parameterize consciously*: Set temperature, top-p, and max-tokens appropriately for the task; choose low values for facts, higher for creativity.
10. *Plan agentically*: Encourage the model to check intermediate steps, use tools, and only finish when a complete solution is reached.
11. *Outsource calculations*: Have the model generate code when exact counting or calculation tasks are required.
12. *Create metaprompts*: Have the AI itself generate suggestions for optimal prompts (Prompting for Prompts).

Don'ts

1. *Avoid blind trust*: Do not rely solely on the knowledge stored in the model—always verify facts through external, reliable sources.
2. *Do not omit examples*: Under no circumstances should you forgo representative examples or step-by-step instructions for critical or complex tasks.
3. *Do not misuse the model*: Do not let complex calculations take place solely "in the head" of the LLM; instead, shift them to explicitly generated code or suitable tools.
4. *Do not ignore hallucination risks*: Do not accept unchecked references without filtering.
5. *Demand iterative revision*: Do not forgo iterative revision; instead, require review, self-critique, and, if necessary, multi-stage revisions from the language model.

References

Brown, T. B., Mann, B., Ryder, N., Subbiah, M., Kaplan, J., Dhariwal, P., Neelakantan, A., Shyam, P., Sastry, G., Askell, A., Agarwal, S., Herbert-Voss, A., Krueger, G., Henighan, T., Child, R., Ramesh, A., Ziegler, D. M., Wu, J., & Winter, C., et al. (2020). Language Models are few-shot learners. In *Proceedings of the 34th international conference on neural information processing systems (NIPS)* (pp. 1877–1901) https://dl.acm.org/doi/abs/10.5555/3495724.3495883.

Deng, Y., Zhang, W., Chen, Z., & Gu, Q. (2024). *Rephrase and respond: Let large language models ask better questions for themselves*. https://arxiv.org/abs/2311.04205v2.

Dhuliawala, S., Komeili, M., Xu, J., Raileanu, R., Li, X., Celikyilmaz, A., & Weston, J. (2024). Chain-of-Verification reduces hallucination in Large Language Models. *Findings of the Association for Computational Linguistics: ACL, 2024*, 3563–3578.

Dong, Q., Li, L., Dai, D., Zheng, C., Ma, J., Li, R., Xia, H., Xu, J., Wu, Z., Chang, B., Sun, X., & Sui, Z. (2024). A survey on in-context learning. In *Proceedings of the 2024 conference on empirical methods in natural language processing (EMNLP)*, 1107–1128. https://doi.org/10.18653/v1/2024.emnlp-main.64.

Giray, L. (2023). Prompt engineering with ChatGPT: A guide for academic writers. *Annals of biomedical engineering, 51*(12), 2629–2633. https://doi.org/10.1007/s10439-023-03272-4.

Heiser, A. (2024). *Texten mit ChatGPT. Springer Fachmedien Wiesbaden.* https://doi.org/10.1007/978-3-658-45601-6.

Huang, L., Yu, W., Ma, W., Zhong, W., Feng, Z., Wang, H., Chen, Q., Peng, W., Feng, X., Qin, B., & Liu, T. (2025). A survey on hallucination in Large Language Models: Principles, taxonomy, challenges, and open questions. *ACM Transactions on Information Systems, 43*(2), 1–55. https://doi.org/10.1145/3703155.

Kessler, E. H., & Bailey, J. R. (Eds.). (2007). *Handbook of organizational and managerial wisdom*. SAGE.

Kojima, T., Gu, S. S., Reid, M., Matsuo, Y., & Iwasawa, Y. (2022). Large Language Models are zero-shot reasoners. In *36th Conference on neural information processing systems (NeurIPS 2022)*.

Lewis, P., Perez, E., Piktus, A., Petroni, F., Karpukhin, V., Goyal, N., Küttler, H., Lewis, M., Yih, W., Rocktäschel, T., Riedel, S., & Kiela, D. (2020). Retrieval-augmented generation for knowledge-intensive NLP tasks. In H. Larochelle, M. Ranzato, R. Hadsell, M. F. Balcan, & H. Lin (Eds.), *Advances in neural information processing systems* (vol. 33, pp. 9459–9474). Curran Associates, Inc.

MacCallum, N., & Lee, J. (2025, June 26th). *GPT-4.1 Prompting Guide*. OpenAI. https://cookbook.openai.com/examples/gpt4-1_prompting_guide.

Meskó, B. (2023). Prompt engineering as an important emerging skill for medical professionals: Tutorial. *Journal of Medical Internet Research, 25*, e50638. https://doi.org/10.2196/50638.

Nguyen, M.-T., Nguyen, D.-H., Sabahi, S., Le Hung, Yang, J., & Hotta, H. (2023). *When giant language brains just aren't enough! Domain pizzazz with knowledge sparkle dust*. https://arxiv.org/abs/2305.07230v2.

Patil, R., & Gudivada, V. (2024). A review of current trends, techniques, and challenges in Large Language Models (LLMs). *Applied Sciences, 14*(5), 2074. https://doi.org/10.3390/app14052074.

Press, O., Zhang, M., Min, S., Schmidt, L., Smith, N., & Lewis, M. (2023). Measuring and narrowing the compositionality gap in language models. In H. Bouamor, J. Pino, & K. Bali (Eds.), *Findings of the Association for Computational Linguistics: EMNLP 2023* (pp. 5687–5711). Association for Computational Linguistics. https://doi.org/10.18653/v1/2023.findings-emnlp.378.

Reynolds, L., & McDonell, K. (2021). Prompt programming for Large Language Models: Beyond the few-shot paradigm. *CHI Conference on Human Factors in Computing Systems*, Article No. 314. https://doi.org/10.1145/3411763.3451760.

Sahoo, P., Singh, A. K., Saha, S., Jain, V., Mondal, S., & Chadha, A. (2025). *A systematic survey of prompt engineering in large language models: Techniques and applications*. https://arxiv.org/abs/2402.07927v2.

Shi, Z., & Lipani, A. (2024). *DePT: Decomposed prompt tuning for parameter-efficient fine-tuning*. https://arxiv.org/abs/2309.05173v5.

Singh, A., Ehtesham, A., Kumar, S., & Khoei, T. T. (2024). Enhancing AI systems with agentic workflows patterns in Large Language Model. In *In 2024 IEEE World AI IoT Congress (AIIoT)* (pp. 527–532). IEEE. https://doi.org/10.1109/AIIoT61789.2024.10578990.

Steinmann, N., & Piazza, A. (2024). KI-basierte Textkreation im Content Marketing: Design und Evaluation eines effektiven Prompts. *HMD Praxis der Wirtschaftsinformatik, 61*(2), 402–417. https://doi.org/10.1365/s40702-024-01058-3.

Wang, X., Wei, J., Schuurmans, D., Le, Q., Chi, E., Narang, S., Chowdhery, A., & Zhou, D. (2023). Self-consistency improves chain of thought reasoning in Language Models. In *International conference on Learning Representations (ICLR)*. Online First. https://doi.org/10.48550/arXiv.2203.11171.

Wei, J., Wang, X., Schuurmans, D., Bosma, M., Ichter, B., Xia, F., Chi, E., Le, Q., & Zhou, D. (2023). Chain-of-Thought prompting elicits reasoning in Large Language Models. In *36th Conference on neural information processing systems (NeurIPS 2022)*.

Xu, R., & Peng, J. (2025). *A comprehensive survey of deep research: Systems, methodologies, and applications*. https://arxiv.org/abs/2506.12594v1.

Yao, S., Yu, D., Zhao, J., Shafran, I., Griffiths, T. L., Cao, Y., & Narasimhan, K. (2023). *Tree of thoughts: Deliberate problem solving with large language models*. https://arxiv.org/abs/2305.10601v2.

Yu, W., Zhang, H., Pan, X., Ma, K., Wang, H., & Yu, D. (2024). Chain-of-Note: Enhancing robustness in retrieval-augmented Language Models. In *Proceedings of the 2024 conference on empirical methods in natural language processing*.

Zheng, H. S., Mishra, S., Chen, X., Cheng, H.-T., Chi, E. H., Le, V. Q., & Zhou, D. (2024). *Take a step back: Evoking reasoning via abstraction in large language models*. https://arxiv.org/abs/2310.06117v2.

Zuckarelli, J. L. (2025). *Programmieren mit ChatGPT*. Springer. https://doi.org/10.1007/978-3-662-69433-6.

Documentation: Maintaining Academic Integrity

4

Abstract

This chapter addresses the requirements and forms of documentation when using artificial intelligence (AI) in academic work. It first describes the principles of responsible AI use—transparency and labeling, accountability and expert oversight, as well as ethical, fair, and legal use—and situates these within the context of scientific integrity. It then presents current regulations from leading scientific publishers, particularly the clear distinction between assistive and generative AI, requirements for disclosure, and the handling of biases in AI-generated content. The chapter explains various forms of documentation, ranging from holistic and tool-oriented to work-phase-oriented, reflection-oriented documentation, and AI cards. Each form of documentation is contextualized in terms of its purpose, application, and practical examples. The aim of this chapter is to present principles and practice-oriented forms of documenting AI use in order to safeguard scientific integrity in research.

"Technology is a useful servant, but a dangerous master."
– Christian Lange (1921, Section IV)

4.1 Principles of AI Use

The responsible use of AI in academic work is the subject of intense discussion and numerous guidelines. For example, the German Research Foundation (DFG) published a statement on AI in 2023. In parallel, the European Commission is developing dynamic guidelines as part of the European Research Area Platform (2025). The German Ombudsman for Scientific Integrity has also addressed key aspects of dealing with AI (Frisch, 2024; Frisch et al., 2023). These approaches are complemented by recommendations from expert working groups as well as relevant scientific publications.

F. Lang, *Using Artificial Intelligence in Term Papers and Theses*,
https://doi.org/10.1007/978-3-662-73208-3_4

The following presents the most important principles that enable a structured and responsible approach to AI in research.

4.1.1 Scientific Integrity

In order to use AI responsibly in academic work, it is first necessary to clarify what scientific integrity actually means. An important point of reference is the European Code of Conduct for Research Integrity, published by ALLEA (All European Academies, the federation of European academies of sciences) in 2017. This document formulates four fundamental principles for scientific integrity (ALLEA, 2017), as shown in Fig. 4.1.

These four fundamental principles form the basis of good scientific practice and apply regardless of whether AI is used in the research process or not. Reliability here means that research must be conducted carefully, methodically sound, and in a way that is traceable. Honesty obliges authors to present all contributions in the research process openly and transparently, i.e., sources, support, and work processes must be fairly and fully documented. Respect refers to the responsible treatment of contributors, colleagues, society, as well as cultural and natural foundations of life. Finally, the principle of accountability requires researchers to take responsibility for all phases of their work—from the idea, through implementation, to publication.

The following principles for the use of AI are derived from these universally valid fundamental principles.

4.1.2 Principle 1: Transparency and Disclosure

A cornerstone of responsible AI use in academia is transparency and disclosure, as the use of AI must, in principle, be made explicit. This particularly concerns texts,

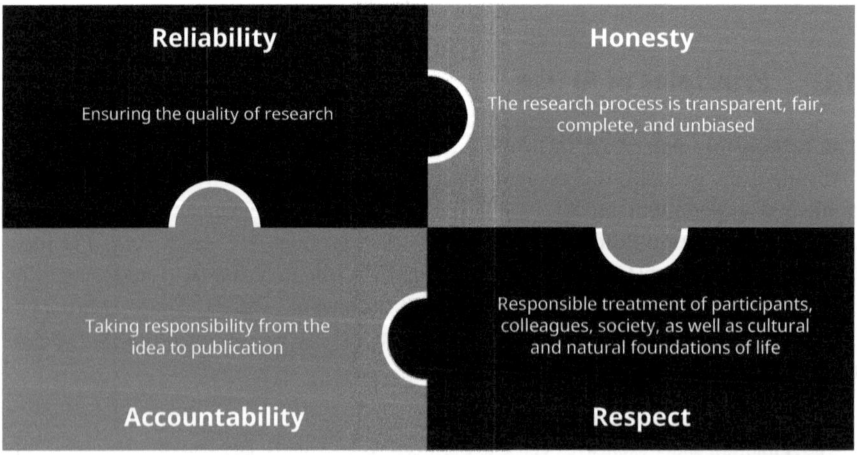

Fig. 4.1 Core principles of the European Code of Conduct for Research Integrity. (ALLEA, 2017)

results, or other content generated with the help of AI. It must be comprehensible to external third parties which AI tool was used, in what way, and for what purpose (DFG, 2023).

As Frisch et al. (2023) emphasize, these requirements are derived directly from the guidelines for ensuring good scientific practice of the German Research Foundation (DFG, 2024). For example, Guideline 1 of the Code emphasizes the obligation to "strict honesty with regard to one's own and third-party contributions"—a demand that is particularly relevant for AI-generated content. Guideline 7 requires, as part of quality assurance, the transparent disclosure of all materials used in the research process, including software. In addition, Guideline 12 calls for comprehensive documentation of all relevant information to make scientific results comprehensible and replicable.

Disclosure is not just about declaring the mere use of AI. What matters is the extent to which AI has significantly influenced the result (Blau et al., 2024). Only if the AI's contribution is substantively relevant, for example in generating or structuring scientific arguments, is there an obligation to disclose. Basic supportive functions such as spell-checking or grammar correction are not subject to these requirements (European Research Area Platform, 2025), as they do not shape the scientific result in terms of content.

Transparency in documentation is therefore more than a technical footnote: it is an expression of scientific accountability.

4.1.3 Principle 2: Responsibility and Informed Control

Assuming final responsibility for the result is also an expression of scientific accountability. Even if individual components were created or supported using AI tools, responsibility for the accuracy and integrity of the content remains entirely with the respective author (European Research Area Platform, 2025).

This means that all content generated by AI must be critically reviewed: for factual accuracy, argumentative precision, and logical conclusions (Blau et al., 2024). This includes, in particular, the careful checking of quotations and paraphrases, since AI systems can generate plausible-sounding references that are not always correct. The underlying literature must therefore always be independently researched and verified (Frisch et al., 2023). Furthermore, it must be taken into account that AI-generated content can contain biases, may produce so-called hallucinations or factual inaccuracies, and may reproduce outdated information (Oertner, 2024). These risks require a conscious, reflective, and verifiable engagement with all AI-supported work steps.

However, this responsibility can only be met if one understands how AI systems work. Researchers—as well as students—must also have a technical understanding of the underlying processes in order to critically evaluate, contextualize, and methodologically question results. Simply adopting AI-generated content without a sound understanding contradicts the principles of scientific integrity. Therefore, it is not sufficient to simply delegate tasks to AI. Rather, the systems must be used purposefully, appropriately, and with the necessary expertise (Frisch et al., 2023). Especially because the field of artificial intelligence is developing so rapidly, it is important to engage continuously with the technology. Anyone using AI in academic work should not only understand the basic functioning but also be willing to engage in ongoing learning—about new tools, applications, and potential risks. Only in this way can it be ensured that results developed with AI truly meet the requirements of scientific quality and integrity (European Research Area Platform, 2025).

4.1.4 Principle 3: Ethical, Fair, and Legal Use

The goal of research is to create knowledge that benefits society. The use of AI can significantly advance this goal, whether through increased efficiency, new methodological possibilities, or innovative insights. At the same time, however, the technology also poses societal risks, such as the reproduction of biases or a lack of transparency in the creation of scientific content. Such risks cannot be ignored but must be actively addressed in order to uphold the standards of responsible science. Against this background, it is recommended to establish ethical guidelines for dealing with AI, which serve as a framework for morally relevant questions (Blau et al., 2024).

In principle, the use of AI systems in academia must be compatible with four central ethical principles (HLEG AI, 2019):

1. Respect for human autonomy
2. Prevention of harm
3. Fairness
4. Explainability

First and foremost, human autonomy must be preserved, i.e., people must be able to exercise self-determination when interacting with AI and be protected from manipulation or paternalism. With regard to the prevention of harm, AI systems must not cause physical or psychological harm, must be designed to be safe and robust, and must take into account and protect vulnerable groups from misuse. Fairness is also a crucial principle, meaning the equitable distribution of opportunities and risks, protection from discrimination, as well as transparency and explainability of AI decisions. This means that users must be able to understand and, if necessary, challenge decisions, with the degree of required explainability depending on the specific application context (HLEG AI, 2019).

In addition to ethical responsibility, legal and regulatory requirements must also be observed when using AI in research. Data protection and intellectual property rights are particularly relevant here. For example, personal data may not be entered into AI systems without explicit consent, especially if these systems are designed to further process the data or use it for model training (European Research Area Platform, 2025). Copyright issues also play an important role. Language models can, under certain circumstances, reproduce protected texts—for example, by reproducing entire passages from books, articles, or online sources. If this occurs without proper disclosure or citation, it formally constitutes plagiarism

(Henderson et al., 2023). Students and researchers must therefore be particularly careful to check whether AI-generated content actually represents their own work or unintentionally reproduces someone else's intellectual property.

At the same time, the legal framework is constantly evolving: With the EU AI Act, the European Union (2024b) has created a comprehensive legal framework for the use of AI. However, Article 2(6) of this law explicitly exempts scientific research from the strict regulations of the Act. According to Recital 25 (European Union, 2024a), this exemption is intended to protect scientific progress and safeguard academic freedom. At the same time, it is emphasized that research activities must still be conducted within recognized ethical and professional standards. This means that, even if research is not directly subject to the full regulation of the EU AI Act, this does not relieve scientists and students of their responsibility to comply with legal requirements and ethical principles.

4.1.5 Summary of Principles

The principles developed above mark the central guidelines for the responsible use of AI in academic work. They clarify the requirements that transparency, assumption of responsibility, and ethical and legal frameworks must generally meet in the academic context. It becomes clear that while AI can be used as a support, scientific responsibility always remains with the human. Figure 4.2 provides an overview of the key aspects underlying the three principles.

The three principles do not stand in isolation but interact to ensure the integrity of AI use in academic practice. The guidelines presented for AI use are not additional or separate rules, but rather specify and translate the fundamental principles of scientific integrity explained at the outset to address new technological challenges. In other words: The principles for AI use apply the general standards of good scientific practice in an AI-specific context and thus clarify what is important when AI is to be used meaningfully, responsibly, and in compliance with regulations in study and research. Table 4.1 shows how the individual principles relate to the four fundamental principles.

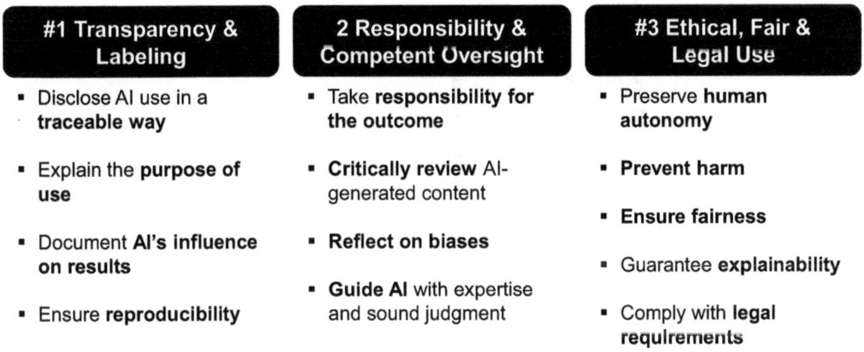

Fig. 4.2 Overview of the three principles of AI use

Table 4.1 Principles for AI Use and Fundamental Principles of Scientific Integrity

Fundamental Principle/Principle	Reliability	Honesty	Respect	Accountability
1. Transparency & Disclosure	Enables verifiability and reproducibility	Honest disclosure of the AI component prevents intentional and unintentional deception	Appreciation through transparency and openness towards all involved	Makes process and result comprehensible, creates a basis for accountability
2. Responsibility & Informed Control	Ensures quality and accuracy through critical review and conscious control of AI results	Truthfulness in the presentation and independent review of all content, minimizes risks of unintentional deception	Diligence towards contributors and readers, recognition of the limits of AI	Full final responsibility remains with the human, conscious control and oversight of the entire process
3. Ethical, Fair & Legal Use	Promotes reliability through consistent adherence to ethical and legal standards	Integrity in application, results are thus fair and unbiased	Ensures respectful treatment by avoiding discrimination and violation of rights	Responsible handling of risks and consequences in light of legal and ethical standards

4.2 Current Regulations at Publishers in Research

Adhering to the principles of good scientific practice is indispensable both in research and in academic study. The standards that apply in professional research must therefore also be binding in student work. This also concerns the handling of new technologies such as AI in the form of language models.

4.2.1 Overview

In research, scientific findings are predominantly published in academic journals and at scientific conferences. The academic publishers responsible for this have increasingly commented on the role of AI applications in recent years. Table 4.2 provides an overview of the regulations of the five largest scientific publishers (Elsevier, Wiley, Springer, Taylor & Francis, and SAGE), which together account for over half (and even 70% in the social sciences) of all scientific publications (Larivière et al., 2015). The guidelines sometimes distinguish between supportive and generative AI. Supportive AI refers to applications that optimize existing, human-created content. This includes AI-based spelling and grammar checks, style improvements, or tools for simplifying language. In contrast, generative AI such as LLMs are capable of independently generating new content. This includes not only original texts, but also translations, summaries, or the creation of images and tables (Elsevier, 2025; SAGE, 2025).

4.2.2 AI Authorship

Despite the currently inconsistent regulations regarding the handling of AI-generated content, there is consensus among the major scientific publishers on one central point: Artificial intelligence—including generative language models such as ChatGPT—cannot assume scientific authorship. This unanimous position became necessary especially after the rapid rise of generative AI in 2022, as some authors attempted to list AI systems as co-authors in scientific publications.

Such a step, however, contradicts the fundamental principles of scientific authorship. Only those who make an original, traceable contribution, give their consent to the final version, and assume responsibility for the outcome can be considered an author (Guideline 14, DFG, 2024). AI can neither give consent to publication nor assume responsibility for the results, so AI is to be regarded solely as a tool and not as an author or co-author.

4.2.3 Text Generation

Whether AI may be used for text generation in a scientific context depends largely on the distinction between supportive and generative use. All major scientific

Table 4.2 Overview of AI regulations at the five major scientific publishers

	Elsevier (2025)	Springer (2025)	Wiley (2025)	Taylor & Francis (2025)	SAGE (2025)
AI as Author	Not permitted	Not permitted	Not permitted	Not permitted	Not permitted
AI as Writing Aid	Supportive only, no original texts	Generally permitted under human control	Generally permitted under human control	Generally permitted under human control	Generally permitted under human control
AI-generated Images	Generally not permitted	Generally not permitted	Concept diagrams permitted, factual illus-trations not	Not permitted in general	Generally not permitted
Bias Review	Warning about pos-sible biases	Warning about possible biases	Obligation to check for biases	Warning about pos-sible biases	Obligation to check for biases
Disclosure & Transparency	General obligation to disclose	Disclosure required if use exceeds assistance	Disclosure required if use exceeds assistance	General obligation to disclose	Disclosure required if use exceeds assistance
Responsibility	Exclusively the human	Exclusively the human	Exclusively the human	Exclusively the human	Exclusively the human

publishers permit the use of supportive AI—for example, for linguistic editing, stylistic refinement, or improving readability based on a human-written text. The substantive responsibility clearly remains with the authors.

Provided that the human controls the writing process, reviews the content, and assumes full scientific responsibility, many publishers also allow more extensive use of generative AI—that is, the use of AI to create original text passages. Nevertheless, such use is not recommended without reservation, as it places increased demands on transparency, verifiability, and documentation. Regardless of the degree of AI use, the responsibility for factual accuracy, contextualization, and adherence to scientific integrity always remains with the human.

4.2.4 Image Generation

As a rule, many of the major publishers prohibit the use of images that have been created entirely by AI or substantially altered by it. This particularly concerns generative image models that rely on training data for which rights transfers have not yet been conclusively clarified. A frequently cited reason for this restrictive stance is copyright concerns: Since many AI models are trained on copyrighted image material, there is concern that works created from them may constitute legal infringements or lead to future compensation claims (Elsevier, 2025; Springer, 2025). The legal questions of whether creators must be compensated for the use of their works in AI training and who ultimately owns the rights to the generated content have not yet been conclusively resolved (Chesterman, 2025). In addition, numerous publishers require their authors to carefully review the terms of use of the AI platforms they employ and to pay attention to the transfer of usage rights.

At the same time, defined exceptions exist: In particular, when AI-generated images are themselves the subject of scientific investigation—for example, in studies analyzing human perception of artificially generated visual worlds—their use is explicitly permitted. Technical adjustments for purely visual optimization, such as brightness or contrast corrections, are also considered permissible by Elsevier, for example, as long as the scientific content of the illustration remains unchanged.

A look at specific publisher policies, however, also reveals the current lack of uniformity. For instance, SAGE generally permits the use of such images, but attaches certain conditions, mainly requirements for transparency and disclosure. Wiley is also open to the use of AI-generated images, provided they are used to illustrate abstract or conceptual content—such as flowcharts, model sketches, or structural overviews—and their accuracy can be verified in the scientific context. In contrast, Taylor & Francis prohibits the use of AI-generated image content altogether, regardless of the intended purpose.

4.2.5 Biases

Since language models are trained on large amounts of text data, which themselves may contain social stereotypes, prejudices, or structural biases, there is a risk that AI-generated content will reproduce these so-called biases. This can result in the uncritical reinforcement of discriminatory patterns—such as racist or sexist stereotypes—or in certain groups being systematically underrepresented in scientific presentations.

Against this background, the author guidelines of all major scientific publishers now contain clear instructions on how to deal with possible biases in AI-generated texts. These range from warnings about potential biases to concrete obligations to check for them. In the case of Wiley and SAGE, the publishers explicitly require authors not only to verify factual accuracy, but also to critically review the substantive balance, representativeness, and social appropriateness of AI-generated content.

4.2.6 Disclosure & Transparency

With regard to documenting the use of AI, publishers have generally formulated clear requirements and explicitly demand disclosure of the use of generative AI. A distinction is often made between generative and supportive AI. The latter—such as correction suggestions or grammar checks—do not require separate documentation at Springer, Wiley, or SAGE, for example. Disclosure notes are usually integrated directly into the scientific text, for example in the methodology section, or in a separate paragraph on AI use, which is placed before or appended to the main text.

Wiley, in particular, imposes far-reaching requirements. In addition to a note in the published text, authors must already provide a detailed breakdown when submitting the manuscript. Specifically, they are to indicate which passages were supported by AI, which AI tools and versions were used, for what purpose they were employed, how the results were verified, and whether the AI influenced the argumentative structure or the conclusions of the text. This information is then subject to editorial review.

In summary, the publishers' guidelines make it clear that transparent disclosure of AI use is a central expression of scientific integrity. It provides the necessary basis for traceability and verifiable quality assurance, thereby strengthening the trustworthiness of scientific work. At the same time, it promotes the integration into scientific discourse by revealing the extent to which technological tools have contributed to knowledge generation. In a research landscape increasingly shaped by AI, this transparency becomes a prerequisite for responsible and credible science.

4.2.7 Responsibility

The regulations on the responsibility of authors also serve as a concise summary of current publisher guidelines: All major scientific publishers regard artificial intelligence as a mere tool—not as an autonomous creator or co-author of scientific content. Full responsibility for all content, regardless of whether it was produced by human hand or with the help of AI, remains entirely with the authors. It is not sufficient for statements to appear formally correct; they must also be scientifically substantiated, coherent, and appropriate in context.

In addition, the specific risks associated with the use of generative AI must also be actively considered. These include, in particular, so-called hallucinations as well as structural biases. The latter also demonstrate that the use of AI in a scientific context does not relieve one of ethical responsibility. On the contrary: The more powerful the systems, the greater the need to question, contextualize, and, if necessary, correct their results in light of scientific and societal standards.

Only through responsible and transparent use of AI tools can trust in science be maintained. Integrity, accountability, and ethical reflection remain—especially in the age of AI—indispensable prerequisites for scientific work.

4.3 Forms of Documentation

For term papers and theses, the documentation of AI use is of particular importance. How exactly this documentation should be carried out depends—not only on the principles explained above—but also on the requirements of the respective supervisor. It is therefore advisable to consult with them. In some cases, there are specific guidelines from the supervisors or the university that must be strictly followed. Where such requirements are lacking, it is the responsibility of the students to disclose their use of AI in a transparent, honest, and appropriate manner. The documentation can take different forms, depending on the purpose it is intended to serve. The most important variants of these documentation forms and their respective functions are presented in the remainder of this section.

4.3.1 Different Forms of Documentation with Various Objectives

Depending on the objective and scope, different forms of documentation can be distinguished, each with its own focus—such as structure, level of detail, or reflection. Table 4.3 systematically presents the key forms of documentation for the use of AI in student papers. The overview follows the classification by Baresel et al. (2024), supplemented by Wahle et al. (2023), and shows which type of documentation is suitable for which purpose and which content is emphasized in each case.

Table 4.3 Overview of Documentation Forms

Form of Documentation	Description	Strengths	Weaknesses
Holistic Documentation	Comprehensive, narrative account of AI use throughout the course of the work	Time-efficient, provides an overview of the entire process, meets transparency requirements	Low level of detail, limited depth of reflection
Tool-Oriented Documentation	Lists software and AI tools used, including their purpose and scope	Clear technical overview, easy to create	Lacks context for tool selection, no critical reflection
Work-Phase-Oriented Documentation	Documents AI use by work phase, including degree of intensity	Shows phase and degree of use, promotes reflection and traceability	More effort required, ongoing documentation necessary
Documentation via AI Cards	Standardized template with fixed blocks for AI use throughout the research process	Highly structured, consistent recording of all phases, supports transparency	Rigid template, requires online generator or LaTeX skills
Reflection-Oriented Documentation	Captures personal learning and skill development in dealing with AI	Very deep reflection, promotes critical self-observation, suitable for AI literacy learning objectives	Very time-consuming, high effort, only meaningful with explicit learning objectives

4.3.2 Holistic Documentation

Holistic documentation, as described by Baresel et al. (2024), aims to present the use of AI in the overall context of the academic work. Unlike a mere listing of tools or functions used, this form of documentation emphasizes a coherent, narrative account: How was AI used? For what purpose? In what sequence? And why in this particular way?

This form of presentation is based on the standard research practice of method description and is particularly suitable when AI is used not just at isolated points, but across several phases of the work. In both student and published academic works, holistic documentation is usually found in the methods chapter or as a brief explanatory section before or after the main text. It should also include a clear statement that the principles of good academic practice have been consistently observed—for example, with regard to independent work, citation, and critical reflection on AI use.

A key advantage of holistic documentation is that it does not require laborious logging of individual prompts or AI results. Instead, it allows for an overview that is concise yet meaningful, describing the use of AI throughout the entire process of the work. This makes it comparatively simple and time-efficient to produce. At the same time, holistic documentation meets core requirements for academic transparency and responsibility. An example of holistic documentation can be found in Table 4.4.

4.3.3 Tool-Oriented Documentation

In tool-oriented documentation (Baresel et al., 2024), the focus is on the specific software tools and AI applications used. The aim of this form is to clearly set out which specific programs or services were used, to what extent, and for what purpose in the work process.

Table 4.4 Example of Holistic Documentation

In the context of this academic work, I used various AI-supported software as an aid. During the **topic development** phase, I used ChatGPT to first narrow down the subject area and then refine the research question. Through iterative dialogue with the tool, different questions emerged, which I critically evaluated and formulated in my own words. For the **development of relevant keywords** for the literature search, I used DeepSeek R1. The final selection of keywords was made independently, based on my own professional judgment. For the **transcription** of the conducted interviews, I used Whisper. After automated transcription, I carefully compared all texts with the original recordings. During the **writing process,** I used Grammarly to improve the linguistic accuracy and stylistic clarity of my text. The **principles of good academic practice** were observed at all stages. In particular, I ensured that all AI-generated content was critically reviewed, revised, and not adopted unfiltered, that I always prioritized my own judgment and sense of responsibility, and that all sources and tools used were properly cited.

Table 4.5 Example of Tool-Oriented Documentation

Tool	Version	Purpose	Function Used	Description of Use/ Application Area
Adobe ECharts	6.0	Interactive data visualization	Creation of interactive diagrams and charts	Visualization of analysis results from R
ChatGPT	GPT-4o	Topic development	Generation of topic ideas and research questions	Chat to narrow down the subject area and refine the research question
DeepSeek R1	R1-0528	Keyword identification	Creation of relevant keyword lists	Support for literature research by suggesting search terms
Grammarly	6.15.1	Language correction and style	Grammar and style checking	Improvement of linguistic accuracy and stylistic clarity
R	4.5.0	Data analysis and statistics	Data preparation, statistical calculations	Analysis of standardized questions
Whisper	v3	Transcription of interviews	Automatic speech recognition and transcription	Transcription of conducted interviews, followed by comparison of texts with original recordings

Here, AI tools are documented alongside traditional academic software solutions—such as statistical software like SPSS or R, programming environments like Visual Studio, or specialized scientific programs. All programs whose use is not considered self-evident are recorded. Standard programs such as Microsoft Word or reference management software like Citavi or Zotero, on the other hand, generally do not need to be listed separately, as their use is assumed to be standard in academic writing.

A disadvantage of this form of documentation is its functional-technical orientation: it does not provide information about the considerations that led to the choice of a particular tool, nor about the specific context of use. It also remains unclear whether and to what extent the results produced were critically reviewed. Thus, tool-oriented documentation provides transparency about technical use, but remains comparatively superficial in terms of reflection and evaluation of AI use.

A fictional example is shown in Table 4.5.

4.3.4 Work-Phase-Oriented Documentation

Work-phase-oriented documentation (Baresel et al., 2024) focuses on the timing and content of AI use throughout the academic work process. In contrast to tool-oriented documentation, which centers on the programs used, the focus here is on embedding AI use within the individual work phases. For this, the work phases of one's own project must be clearly named—such as topic selection, literature research, conceptualization, analysis, or writing phase. Within this structure, it must be recorded whether and how AI was used in each phase. It is important that documentation is carried out alongside the work process. Retrospective reconstruction is often incomplete or error-prone, especially if AI use was not systematically recorded.

A key element of this form of documentation is indicating the degree of use, i.e., the intensity of AI involvement. Based on the formulation aid from the Writing Center at Goethe University Frankfurt (2025), which in turn is based on the framework by Rowland (2023), four levels are distinguished, for example:

1. **For inspiration**: AI is used to obtain initial ideas for, e.g., topics or formulations, without replacing one's own text.
2. **Supplementary**: AI is used to clarify specific questions, obtain suggestions for structure, or receive summaries.
3. **Supportive**: AI is used in the development and revision of the text, for example through suggestions or feedback.
4. **Content-shaping**: AI takes on essential tasks such as generating content, outlines, or text sections that are directly adopted.

This form of documentation serves not only transparency but also as evidence of independent academic achievement. It shows in which specific steps AI was used and how much the generated content influenced the final result. In addition, it creates space for reflection. Students actively engage with how and to what extent they used AI as support, thus developing a more conscious understanding of their own work process. Work-phase-oriented documentation therefore not only promotes external traceability but also strengthens academic self-responsibility and the ability to critically assess technological tools.

Table 4.6 shows an illustrative example of work-phase-oriented documentation.

4.3.5 Documentation via AI Cards

AI Cards (Wahle et al., 2023) are a concrete proposal for how the use of artificial intelligence in academic work can be systematically and transparently documented. They follow a work-phase-oriented logic and thus offer a structured way to transparently present the use of AI throughout the research process.

The core of AI Cards is a tabular documentation template divided into ten main blocks. Each of these blocks represents a central phase or function in academic work where AI can potentially be used:

1. **Project details** (e.g., information on those responsible, AI models and versions used)
2. **Idea generation** (e.g., AI for developing or expanding research questions)

Table 4.6 Example of Work-Phase-Oriented Documentation

Work Step	For Inspiration	Supplementary	Supportive	Content-Shaping
Finding and Refining the Topic	ChatGPT 4o: Chat to narrow down the subject area and refine the research question	–	–	–
Understanding the Assignment	–	–	–	–
Research	–	DeepSeek R1: Suggestions for relevant keywords for literature search	–	–
Analyzing Literature/Data	–	Whisper: Automatic transcription of interviews	–	MAXQDA AI Assist: Suggestions for initial coding
Planning and Structuring	–	–	–	–
Writing	Claude Sonnet 3.7: Suggestions for precise definitions and formulations	–	Grammarly: Style and grammar suggestions	–
Revising	–	–	Grammarly: Polishing expression and style	–

3. **Literature overview** (e.g., AI-supported research, categorization, or summarization of academic literature)
4. **Methodology** (e.g., support in selecting or optimizing methods)
5. **Experiments** (e.g., planning and adapting study designs)
6. **Writing** (e.g., paraphrasing or stylistic editing)
7. **Presentation** (e.g., creation or improvement of figures)
8. **Programming** (e.g., generation or documentation of source code)
9. **Data** (e.g., support in preparation, analysis, or visualization)
10. **Ethics** (e.g., reflection on possible risks and ensuring responsible use)

Each block of the AI Cards specifies the degree of use. It is distinguished whether the AI was used to create new content or results, to revise existing content or results, or to compare different content or results.

The AI Cards pursue three overarching goals:

1. **Transparency**: Making visible where, how, and for what purpose AI was used
2. **Integrity**: Ensuring that AI-generated content is truthful, fair, and correct
3. **Accountability**: Clearly stating who is accountable for the use of AI in the project

AI Cards can be created using an online form at *ai-cards.org* and then downloaded, for example, as a PDF or image file. Alternatively, a LaTeX template is available, which is suitable for formally demanding academic works.

A disadvantage of AI Cards is their fixed structure: they follow a predefined pattern that covers many typical use scenarios but is not always sufficiently differentiated or flexible. In addition, their creation is tied to certain technical requirements. Either you rely on the online generator or you need appropriate LaTeX skills to fill out the template manually. For students with less technical experience, this can be an additional hurdle.

Despite these limitations, AI Cards offer a systematic and transparent way to document AI use. An example of a completed AI Card is shown in Fig. 4.3.

4.3.6 Reflection-Oriented Documentation

Reflection-oriented documentation (Baresel et al., 2024) differs significantly from the forms presented above, as it does not primarily focus on the technical traceability of AI use, but on personal engagement with one's own skill development in dealing with AI. The central question is what skills and insights students have developed in working with AI systems—for example, in terms of critical evaluation, appropriate application, or methodological understanding. The aim is to reflect on and make transparent the self-set learning objectives in the area of AI literacy. This form of documentation is therefore particularly suitable for courses or assessment formats in which the acquisition of AI skills is explicitly part of the learning objectives.

In practice, reflection-oriented documentation can be implemented, for example, using a learning matrix: based on defined reflection questions or competency grids, individual progress in dealing with AI can be systematically recorded. Another option is a reflection journal, in which students regularly document, for example, their experiences, decisions, and uncertainties during the process. These ongoing entries then serve as the basis for a final reflection on their own learning process.

The advantage of this form of documentation lies in its depth: it not only promotes technical understanding but also strengthens the ability for critical self-observation—a key competence in the reflective use of AI. At the same time, it makes clear that the use of AI is not just a methodological tool, but a learning field that requires conscious engagement and goal orientation. However, the prerequisite for this form is that AI skills are explicitly part of the learning objectives.

AI Usage Card for AI for thesis

PROJECT DETAILS	PROJECT NAME **AI for thesis**	DOMAIN **Paper**	KEY APPLICATION **AI**
CONTACT(S)	NAME(S) **Fabian Lang**	EMAIL(S) **fabian.lang@hs-hannover.de**	AFFILIATION(S) **Hannover University of Applied Sciences**
MODEL(S)	MODEL NAME(S) **ChatGPT**	VERSION(S) **o3, 4.5, 4o**	
IDEATION	GENERATING IDEAS, OUTLINES, AND WORKFLOWS **ChatGPT**	IMPROVING EXISTING IDEAS **ChatGPT**	FINDING GAPS OR COMPARE ASPECTS OF IDEAS
LITERATURE REVIEW	FINDING LITERATURE **ChatGPT**	FINDING EXAMPLES FROM KNOWN LITERATURE OR ADDING LITERATURE FOR EXISTING STATEMENTS **ChatGPT**	COMPARING LITERATURE
METHODOLOGY	PROPOSING NEW SOLUTIONS TO PROBLEMS	FINDING ITERATIVE OPTIMIZATIONS	COMPARING RELATED SOLUTIONS
EXPERIMENTS	DESIGNING NEW EXPERIMENTS	EDITING EXISTING EXPERIMENTS	FINDING, COMPARING, AND AGGREGATING RESULTS
WRITING	GENERATING NEW TEXT BASED ON INSTRUCTIONS	ASSISTING IN IMPROVING OWN CONTENT OR PARAPHRASING RELATED WORK **ChatGPT**	PUTTING OTHER WORKS IN PERSPECTIVE
PRESENTATION	GENERATING NEW ARTIFACTS **ChatGPT**	IMPROVING THE AESTHETICS OF ARTIFACTS	FINDING RELATIONS BETWEEN OWN OR RELATED ARTIFACTS
CODING	GENERATING NEW CODE BASED ON DESCRIPTIONS OR EXISTING CODE	REFACTORING AND OPTIMIZING EXISTING CODE	COMPARING ASPECTS OF EXISTING CODE
DATA	SUGGESTING NEW SOURCES FOR DATA COLLECTION	CLEANING, NORMALIZING, OR STANDARDIZING DATA	FINDING RELATIONS BETWEEN DATA AND COLLECTION METHODS
ETHICS	WHY DID WE USE AI FOR THIS PROJECT? **Expertise Access** **Efficiency / Speed** **Consistency**	WHAT STEPS ARE WE TAKING TO MITIGATE ERRORS OF AI? **Automatic and manual fact checking**	WHAT STEPS ARE WE TAKING TO MINIMIZE THE CHANCE OF HARM OR INAPPROPRIATE USE OF AI? **Consideration of bias & fairness as well as ethical guidelines & compliance**

THE CORRESPONDING AUTHORS VERIFY AND AGREE WITH THE MODIFICATIONS OR GENERATIONS OF THEIR USED AI-GENERATED CONTENT

AI Usage Card v2.0 https://ai-cards.org PDF — BibTeX

Fig. 4.3 Example of an AI Card. (License: CC BY 4.0; Jan Philip Wahle)

4.4 Do's and Don'ts

Do's

1. *Personal responsibility*: Personally ensure the accuracy, logic, and integrity of all results.
2. *Quality assurance*: Systematically verify AI outputs for factual accuracy, sources, and coherence.

3. *Transparency*: Disclose any use of AI that is relevant to the content.
4. *Documentation choice*: Consistently use the appropriate form (holistic, tool-based, phase-based, or AI card-based).
5. *Legal compliance*: Check data protection, copyright, and personal rights before entering any data.
6. *Continuing education*: Stay up to date with technological and policy developments.
7. *Tool status*: Always treat AI as a tool, never as a co-author.

Don'ts

1. *Blind adoption*: Copy unverified AI-generated passages directly into the text.
2. *AI authorship*: List language models or image generators as authors.
3. *Data misuse*: Upload personal or confidential data without consent.
4. *Importing hallucinations*: Use AI-generated fabricated quotes, sources, or facts.
5. *Plagiarism risk*: Use AI-generated texts without clearly declaring their origin and your own contribution.

References

ALLEA. (2017, May 26th). *The European code of conduct for research intregrity*. https://allea.org/code-of-conduct/.

Baresel, K., Eube, C., Knorr, D., Lutter, L., Nys, J. de & Röben, M. (2024). *KI-Gebrauch im Studienkontext dokumentieren*. https://doi.org/10.48548/PUBDATA-1476.

Blau, W., Cerf, V. G., Enriquez, J., Francisco, J. S., Gasser, U., Gray, M. L., Greaves, M., Grosz, B. J., Jamieson, K. H., Haug, G. H., Hennessy, J. L., Horvitz, E., Kaiser, D. I., London, A. J., Lovell-Badge, R., McNutt, M. K., Minow, M., Mitchell, T. M., Ness, S., et al. (2024). Protecting scientific integrity in an age of generative AI. *Proceedings of the National Academy of Sciences of the United States of America, 121*(22), e2407886121. https://doi.org/10.1073/pnas.2407886121.

Chesterman, S. (2025). Good models borrow, great models steal: Intellectual property rights and generative AI. *Policy and Society, 44*(1), 23–37. https://doi.org/10.1093/polsoc/puae006.

DFG. (2023, May 26th). *Statement by the Executive Committee of the Deutsche Forschungsgemeinschaft (DFG, German Research Foundation) on the Influence of Generative Models of Text and Image Creation on Science and the Humanities and on the DFG's Funding Activities*. https://www.dfg.de/230921_statement_executive_committee_ki_ai.

DFG. (2024). *Leitlinien zur Sicherung guter wissenschaftlicher Praxis: Kodex* (Version 1.2). Deutsche Forschungsgemeinschaft (DFG, German Research Foundation).

Elsevier. (2025, May 26th). *Generative AI policies for journals*. https://www.elsevier.com/about/policies-and-standards/generative-ai-policies-for-journals.

European Union. (2024a). *Recital 25 – EU Artificial Intelligence Act*. https://artificialintelligenceact.eu/de/recital/25/.

European Union (2024b). Regulation (EU) 2024/1689 of the European Parliament and of the Council of 13 June 2024 laying down harmonised rules on artificial intelligence and amending certain Union legislative acts (Artificial Intelligence Act). *Office Journal of the European Union* (L 2024/1689). https://eur-lex.europa.eu/eli/reg/2024/1689/oj.

European Research Area Platform. (2025). *Living guidelines on the responsible use of generative AI in research*. European Commission.

Frisch, K. (2024). *FAQ Künstliche Intelligenz und gute wissenschaftliche Praxis.* Ombudsgremium für die wissenschaftliche Integrität in Deutschland. https://doi.org/10.5281/zenodo.14045171.

Frisch, K., Hagenström, F., & Reeg, N. (2023). Textgenerierende KI und gute wissenschaftliche Praxis. *Zeitschrift für Bibliothekswesen und Bibliographie, 70*(6), 326–336. https://doi.org/10.3196/186429502370667.

HLEG AI. (2019). *Ethics guidelines for trustworthy AI.* European Commission.

Henderson, P., Li, X., Jurafsky, D., Hashimoto, T., Lemley, M. A., & Liang, P. (2023). Foundation models and fair use. *Journal of Machine Learning Research, 24*(400), 1–79. http://jmlr.org/papers/v24/23-0569.html.

Larivière, V., Haustein, S., & Mongeon, P. (2015). The oligopoly of academic publishers in the digital era. *PloS one, 10*(6), e0127502. https://doi.org/10.1371/journal.pone.0127502.

Oertner, M. (2024). ChatGPT als Recherchetool? *Bibliotheksdienst, 58*(5), 259–297. https://doi.org/10.1515/bd-2024-0042.

Rowland, D. R. (2023). Two frameworks to guide discussions around levels of acceptable use of generative AI in student academic research and writing. *Journal of Academic Language & Learning, 17*(1), T31–T69.

SAGE. (2025, May 26th). *Artificial intelligence policy.* https://us.sagepub.com/en-us/nam/artificial-intelligence-policy.

Springer. (2025, May 26th). *Artificial intelligence (AI).* https://www.springer.com/us/editorial-policies/artificial-intelligence%2D%2Dai-/25428500.

Taylor & Francis. (2025, May 26th). *AI policy.* https://taylorandfrancis.com/our-policies/ai-policy/.

Writing Center of the Goethe University Frankfurt. (2025, May 26th). *Framework zur Entwicklung von Regeln bei KI-gestützten Schreibprozessen.* https://www.starkerstart.uni-frankfurt.de/149427334.pdf.

Wahle, J. P., Ruas, T., Mohammad, S. M., Meuschke, N. & Gipp, B. (2023). AI usage cards: Responsibly reporting AI-generated content. In *2023 ACM/IEEE Joint Conference on Digital Libraries (JCDL).*

Wiley. (2025, May 26th). *Using AI tools in your writing: A guide for book authors.* https://www.wiley.com/en-us/publish/book/ai-guidelines.

Planning: AI in Conceptualization 5

Abstract

This chapter demonstrates how artificial intelligence (AI) can provide targeted support in planning academic projects—from topic selection to creating a work plan for the exposé. It describes how AI can be used to systematically develop research topics, formulate precise research questions, and select appropriate methods. The focus is on interactive prompts that uncover individual interests, narrow down topics, and examine them scientifically. Using practical scenarios—such as the role of a virtual tutor or research advisor—the chapter explains how AI fosters reflection, structures decision-making processes, and supports students in methodological planning. It also addresses risks such as the uncritical adoption of AI suggestions or the loss of self-reflection. In addition, the chapter provides concrete guidance on developing an outline, choosing a supervisor, and creating a realistic timeline. The aim of the chapter is to make the planning phase of academic work systematic, efficient, and reflective through the targeted use of AI.

"If you fail to prepare you are preparing to fail."
– H. K. Williams (1919, p. 81)

5.1 The Topic as a Starting Point

Finding a topic is a crucial step in writing an academic paper. While topics for term papers are often assigned, students frequently have the opportunity to formulate their own research topic for final theses. This gives students the chance to actively engage with a subject that personally motivates them and encourages them to pursue their interests. Choosing the right topic can therefore make a significant contribution to the success of the paper by maintaining the students'

F. Lang, *Using Artificial Intelligence in Term Papers and Theses*,
https://doi.org/10.1007/978-3-662-73208-3_5

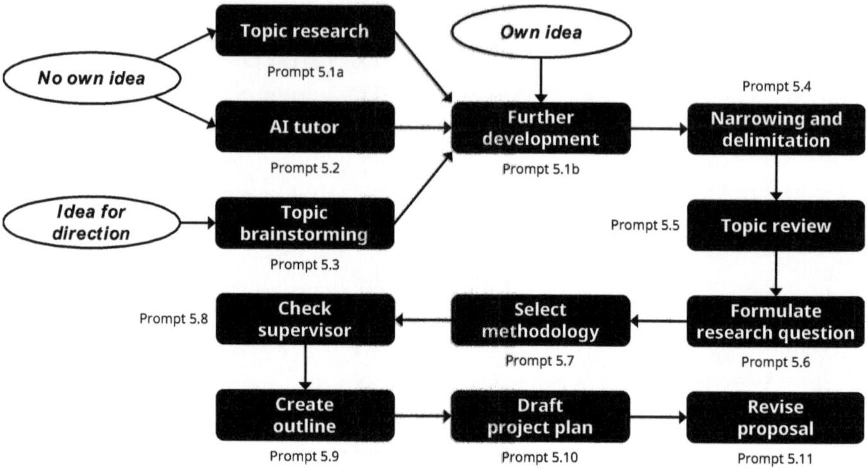

Fig. 5.1 Designing and planning research with AI

motivation throughout the entire process. A well-chosen topic ensures that academic work is not only more productive but also more inspiring, as engaging with a relevant and insightful subject fosters personal enthusiasm and commitment (Kollmann et al., 2016).

Figure 5.1 illustrates the process described in this chapter. It shows how to develop a research topic, derive a research question, and select an appropriate methodology—both with and without an initial idea. This is followed by the search for a supervisor. For this, a meaningful exposé with a well-thought-out structure and a convincing work plan is necessary. For each of these steps, this chapter presents a helpful prompt to support the respective process.

5.2 Finding and Narrowing Down a Topic

This chapter provides an introduction to the criteria and development of a research topic. In addition, it offers concrete recommendations on how AI can be used to generate topic ideas, narrow them down, and assess their suitability.

5.2.1 Research Topic

If the fast-food chain Subway were to list every possible sandwich combination on a menu, it would be about 37 million entries long (Tepper, 2012). This enormous number results from the fact that a sandwich consists of many individual components that can be freely combined, such as different types of bread, fillings, vegetables, sauces, or toppings.

It is similar with research topics: they are composed of several building blocks, which in combination create a unique field of investigation. Typically, a research topic consists of a core aspect under investigation, an explanatory perspective, and one or more delimitations (see examples in Fig. 5.2). Only this targeted combination ensures that an academic paper does not drift into general statements but leads to precise, in-depth, and relevant findings.

Choosing a research topic is therefore like the art of finding the right ingredients for a successful sandwich—not every combination is meaningful or purposeful. The challenge is to combine and narrow down topics so that they are both academically relevant and researchable. The virtually unlimited combinations result in countless potential research questions. The key is to select those that are not only theoretically interesting but also practically feasible.

A suitable topic should not only match personal interests and long-term goals but also meet the requirements of academic methodology. Three central criteria can help in choosing a topic (Pfister, 2021):

1. Resources,
2. Motivation, and
3. Research design.

For a successful paper, there must be sufficient **resources** in the form of high-quality sources or data. The literature base is crucial, as it provides the framework for the research. When choosing a topic, it is important to ensure that the literature is understandable and offers enough material to investigate the research question. In the case of empirical work, the necessary data must also be accessible or collectible. One's own experience or prior work can serve as a source of inspiration.

The choice of topic should not only meet academic requirements but also serve personal **motivation**. It is important to view the topic with academic distance and ensure that personal experiences can also be aligned with theoretical or empirical methods.

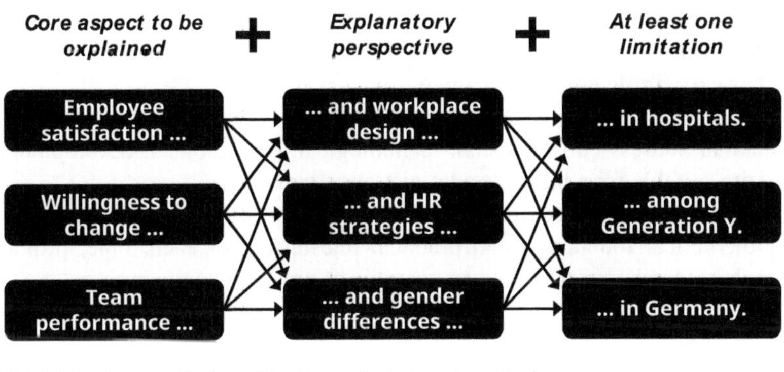

Fig. 5.2 Virtually unlimited combinations when choosing a topic

The **research design** and the associated methodology should, on the one hand, match one's own competence and personal work preferences, but above all be aimed at answering the research question precisely and transparently. A method is not suitable simply because it is familiar or convenient, but because it offers the best possible approach to the research interest in the specific case. The fit between the research question, methodological approach, and individual feasibility is therefore central to the academic quality and practicality of the work.

5.2.2 Developing Topic Ideas

Choosing a suitable topic for a term paper or final thesis can be a challenging task. On the one hand, a topic that is too broad often leads to a multitude of possible directions, making it difficult to focus. On the other hand, it can also be frustrating to find a topic that offers little literature or cannot be sufficiently theoretically substantiated—which can make the work unnecessarily complicated.

If you are lacking ideas, artificial intelligence can help you dive creatively into the subject and find new approaches. It provides useful support for developing initial ideas or further pursuing existing thoughts.

An effective way is to conduct a brainstorming session with AI on various subject areas. You can either start with a completely open approach or further specify an existing idea. In Prompt 5.1, a) a completely open topic search is initiated, where only the discipline (here, for example, human resource management) is known, and b) the brainstorming continues to further develop an existing idea or one gained from the first part.

Prompt 5.1: Brainstorming Topics With and Without an Idea

Context

You are an academically skilled expert with in-depth knowledge of current developments in human resources and broad experience in supervising business administration term papers and theses. Your task is to support me in the structured identification or further development of a research topic.

Instruction

Case a): Topic completely open

Identify ten research topics in the field of human resource management that address current social, technological, or ecological developments and are suitable for a business administration paper.

The topics should be neither too broad nor too narrow, but should allow for theoretical foundation and practical relevance. For each topic, provide sample research questions and an example of practical application.

Case b): Further development of an idea
Identify ten key facets of personnel marketing on social media (e.g., platform-dependent strategies, handling crisis communication, the role of user-generated content) and link each facet with

- appropriate interdisciplinary perspectives (e.g., communication science, data science, occupational psychology),
- current trends in this area,
- two to three possible concrete research questions, and
- a practical example.

Specifications

- Present the results clearly and in a well-structured manner—for example, as a numbered list or table.
- Use precise, academically appropriate language that is easily understandable for students.

In the first variant, ten rather broad topic ideas are generated, which are usually not yet fully developed. However, these can be further elaborated and brought to the right level of abstraction—not too broad, but also not too narrow—through follow-up prompts.

How this can look in practice is shown in the second part of the prompt: In this example, by focusing on personnel marketing on social media, an initial direction is already set. The prompt breaks down the facets of the topic into smaller units of thought, helping to develop a more focused and clearer topic. At the same time, the specific request for interdisciplinary perspectives, current trends, concrete research questions, and practical examples enables a deeper insight into the topic.

This approach can quickly generate an overwhelming amount of information and possibilities, making the decision process more difficult. After all, it is known that a greater choice does not always lead to better decisions. An illustrative example is provided by a study in which participants were asked to select the best search result from a search engine within a short time. When they had only six instead of the usual 24 search results to choose from, the test subjects were not only more satisfied with their decision but also more convinced that they had made the right choice (Oulasvirta et al., 2009). This phenomenon is known as the "Paradox of Choice" (Schwartz, 2016).

Some students also find it difficult to choose a topic and wish for a tutor to support them in their decision. AI can fittingly take on exactly such a role—as shown in Prompt 5.2.

Prompt 5.2: AI as Tutor for Identifying Interests and Topics

Context

You are an experienced master's student in your 10th semester, specializing in human resource management. Your strength is breaking down complex topics in a structured way without offering premature solutions. You act empathetically, patiently, and ask targeted questions to uncover interests, fears, and hidden preferences. Your goal is to help students recognize their own priorities through precise questions—only then do you suggest suitable topics.

Instruction

Step 1—Further field of interest
Start with an open, motivating question about the general area of interest (Example: When you think about your previous seminars: which topic unexpectedly grabbed your attention?).
Step 2—Priorities
Clarify priorities by contrasting options (Example: What is more important to you: a topic with a lot of practical relevance, where you have to collect data, or would you prefer a theoretical analysis?).
Step 3—Fears
Reflect on fears (Example: Where do you see the biggest hurdle? That there is too little literature? Or that the topic will be too dry?).
Step 4—Strengths and weaknesses
Address the person's strengths and weaknesses (Example: Which research methodology do you prefer? More qualitative or quantitative? More theoretical or empirical?).
Offer an interim summary of the findings so far (Example: If I understand you correctly, you would like to ...) and ask whether you should continue asking questions or move on to a final topic suggestion.
Step 5—Topic suggestions
Only now suggest 3 topics that include concrete research questions and practical relevance and are based on the answers. Formulate them so that they cover different levels of abstraction.

Specifications

- Important: After each question, ask a follow-up question that builds on the previous answer.
- Where appropriate, provide answer options that can be answered with "yes/no" or a selection of numbers ("answer option 2").

In this example, the AI takes on the role of an empathetic tutor who guides the student step by step through the process of finding a topic. At the beginning, it asks open, motivating questions to reflect on interests and preferences. It then clarifies which priorities are set through targeted contrasts and gives space to address possible fears or uncertainties. Methodological strengths are also queried to ensure that the chosen topic matches the student's abilities and working style. An interim summary allows the previous answers to be organized and a decision to be made as to whether the process should be deepened or move on to the final topic suggestions. Only when interests and goals are clearly defined does the AI suggest suitable topics.

This approach offers several advantages: it reduces the feeling of being overwhelmed by a multitude of topic options by prioritizing the process of topic selection step by step and structuring it within clear guidelines. At the same time, it actively promotes self-reflection instead of merely presenting lists of topics to choose from. In this way, the AI tutor not only enables the selection of a suitable topic but also a better understanding of one's own interests, strengths, and preferences. This inspiration can also make it easier to come up with other topic ideas beyond those suggested by the AI.

However, there is also a risk: since the AI decides which aspects are considered relevant, potentially interesting topics could be overlooked. In addition, the thematic breadth remains limited, as the focus is strongly oriented toward the previously analyzed preferences and answers.

Another way to find a research topic is to first gain a comprehensive overview of current research debates and industry trends. This makes it possible to identify a broader range of topics and facilitates orientation toward relevant and current issues. It is particularly effective to systematically review current publications to identify exciting developments, controversial discussions, or research gaps that can serve as a starting point for one's own work (Goldenstein et al., 2018; Kollmann et al., 2016).

Prompt 5.3 presents three examples of systematic research on current topic trends. Source material can include, among other things, industry reports (a) from associations or research institutes, which provide valuable insights into current practical challenges and developments. To gain an overview of academic debates, it is also advisable to analyze tables of contents from conference proceedings or academic journals (b), which can be thematically organized. Another example is the evaluation of thesis topics (c), which are often published by university libraries or departments and provide insights into recently addressed research questions.

Prompt 5.3: Topic Inspiration from Trends in a) Practice, b) Research, and c) Teaching

Context

You are an experienced university professor specializing in science analysis, research monitoring, and strategic topic development in the field of business studies. Your task is to systematically evaluate academic and practice-oriented sources such as industry reports, conference proceedings, and theses to identify, classify, and present key topic areas, trends, and research priorities in a structured form. The goal is to develop topic ideas for seminar and final theses.

Instruction

a) **Industry reports**
Please research the last three annual reports of the Organisation Internationale des Constructeurs d'Automobiles (OICA) and ensure that these are available as complete PDF documents. Then analyze the reports to identify the key topics and trends for small and medium-sized enterprises. Present these in order of relevance and support each position with specific excerpts from the sources.

b) **Conferences/Journals**
Analyze the provided table of contents from the proceedings of last year's International Conference on Information Systems (ICIS). Identify the five most frequent main topics, cluster subordinate topic areas into meaningful thematic groups, and for each subtopic, name concrete study examples with their titles.

c) **Theses**
Analyze the provided list of past theses from the institute and identify the dominant topic areas in descending order. Group related thesis titles into meaningful subcategories for each main topic and, for each category, provide concrete examples (thesis titles) with their respective research focuses or questions, if possible.

Specifications

- The presentation should be clear and organized by main topics.
- Sort in order of relevance.
- Whenever possible, provide the source for each excerpt.
- Ensure that your assessment of relevance is transparent and comprehensible—justify your weighting if necessary.

Based on these inspirations, the identified topics can be further developed by refining and specifying them with the help of AI, as in Prompt 5.1. Alternatively, the topics can be brought into the chat with the virtual tutor from Prompt 5.2 to reflect on and expand them together.

5.2.3 Narrowing Down and Reviewing the Topic

In order to efficiently work on a topic for a term paper or thesis, it is crucial to define it clearly and precisely. A topic that is too broad often leads to only superficial treatment, which weakens both the analysis and the results.

A precise narrowing down offers several advantages: complexity is reduced, allowing focus on the essential aspects. At the same time, it enables targeted use

Table 5.1 Options for narrowing down, adapted from Franck (2017)

1. By time	**5. By sources**
... since 2020 ... after reunification ... in the last five years	... on social media ... in annual reports ... in official statistics
2. Geographically	**6. By specific persons/institutions**
... in Berlin ... in Germany ... in Sub-Saharan Africa	... economic theories of Joseph Schumpeter ... market strategy of Amazon ... ECB interest rate policy
3. By institutions	**7. By sub-discipline**
... in start-ups ... in NASDAQ-listed companies ... in public institutions	... financial analysis ... organizational theory analysis ... human resources evaluation
4. By groups of people	**8. By theoretical approach**
... among women ... in Generation X ... among civil servants	... game-theoretical analysis ... institutional economics analysis ... neoclassical synthesis

of time and attention. Additionally, the work becomes more manageable and gains depth and relevance.

There are various approaches to effectively narrow down a topic; Table 5.1 presents eight exemplary possibilities (based on Franck, 2017).

Often, narrowing down a topic requires a combination of different approaches to find the right level of abstraction. By combining several narrowing criteria, a topic can be specified and limited to a specific research area. For example, a topic can be restricted not only geographically, but also by groups of people, theoretical approaches, or other relevant factors.

AI can also assist in narrowing down a topic. It can not only generate examples of possible narrowing approaches, but also evaluate them in advance regarding their suitability. In doing so, it can systematically highlight, among other things, the advantages and disadvantages as well as the practical feasibility. Prompt 5.4 provides an example to support the narrowing of a rather general topic.

Prompt 5.4: Further Narrowing Down a Topic

Context

You are an experienced professor of finance specializing in sustainable finance and empirical capital market research. Your task is to help me, as a student, to specifically narrow down my topic "Green Bonds and Corporate Performance." The goal is to find a precise, research-practically meaningful focus that enables a scientifically sound, feasible, and original thesis.

Instruction
I am interested in the topic "Green Bonds and Corporate Performance" for my thesis.

Please suggest—in descending order of suitability—five meaningful, concrete narrowing criteria (e.g., by time, geography, institutions, groups of people, sources, specific persons/institutions, sub-discipline, theoretical approach) and discuss for each of the five criteria:

1. Advantages (e.g., data availability),
2. Risks (e.g., methodological limitations),
3. Practical feasibility for a candidate (e.g., research effort, access to sources, etc.).

Finally, evaluate each narrowing criterion for its suitability for a qualification thesis.

Specifications

- Present the discussion of the five criteria clearly and provide a summary table at the end.
- Use a traffic light system for the evaluation of the criteria (green = well suited, yellow = conditionally suited, red = less suited) or alternatively a short text rating (e.g., "high," "medium," "low").
- All assessments must refer to the topic "Green Bonds and Corporate Performance."

The three-stage structure of the prompt—suggestions, discussion of criteria, and final evaluation—ensures a clearly traceable decision-making process on a broad basis. At the same time, it allows for consideration of practical aspects such as data access and research effort, as well as keeping methodological risks and scientific requirements in view.

Despite the support provided by AI, the final decision on narrowing down the topic always remains with the student. AI serves only as an aid to highlight possible options and provide structured impulses for thought. There is always a risk that AI, due to limited data or incorrect assessments, may over- or underestimate certain criteria. Therefore, it is important to critically question the AI's suggestions. AI is a tool intended to facilitate the decision-making process—not a substitute for one's own substantive and methodological engagement with the topic. In this sense, the final review of the chosen topic must also be carried out independently and critically questioned. AI can provide valuable impulses and perspectives to support this process. Nevertheless, it remains essential to evaluate the topic oneself based on clear criteria to ensure that it meets the requirements of a scientific paper. Ultimately, responsibility for the quality and relevance of the topic selection always lies with the human.

When reviewing the suitability of a topic, various aspects should be considered. First and foremost, feasibility is crucial: the topic must be realistically achievable, especially with regard to methodology, results, and the time frame. The topic should also be interesting, so that it sparks personal engagement as well as curiosity in academia and practice. Furthermore, the degree of novelty is a key factor: the results should be innovative and not merely reproduce already known findings. An exception is targeted replication studies for precisely this purpose. It must be ensured that the work meets ethical standards and serves the higher goals of science. Finally, the topic should have clear relevance for both academic and practical questions in order to make a meaningful contribution in both areas.

These criteria, known as FINER (according to the initial letters, see table) (Cummings et al., 2013), summarize the essential requirements for a research topic. An overview of the criteria can be found in Table 5.2.

When reviewing a topic, the main question is whether the topic is fundamentally suitable. This includes assessing whether it is feasible within the given time and methodological framework and at the same time offers sufficient depth and relevance. It is equally important to identify possible risks and pitfalls. These include methodological challenges, a focus that is too broad or too narrow, or difficulties in data availability. Such potential obstacles should be recognized and addressed early on. Finally, AI can provide impulses for further development of the topic and help to address weaknesses, develop more precise research questions, or discover alternative perspectives.

An illustrative example of a prompt that uses AI specifically to support a critical review of a topic can be found in Prompt 5.5.

Table 5.2 FINER criteria for a research topic, after Cummings et al. (2013)

A research topic should…
be feasible
… have a sufficient number of data sources available. … have the necessary methodological and subject-specific knowledge. … be achievable in terms of time and finances. … remain manageable in scope.
be interesting
… spark the interest of researchers and practitioners.
be novel
… provide new insights into relationships. … confirm, refute, or expand existing theories. … be able to promote innovations in models, methods, or applications.
be ethical
… comply with ethical standards in research. … not cause conflicts of interest or potential harm.
be relevant
… have practical implications for companies, markets, or policy makers. … be able to influence future research questions or approaches.

Prompt 5.5: Reviewing the Chosen Topic

Context

You act as an experienced academic with many years of experience supervising student papers. You provide targeted, well-founded, and at the same time pragmatic feedback on topic proposals. In doing so, you take into account both academic requirements and practical feasibility. The goal is to reflect on the topic in terms of theoretical foundation, methodological feasibility, and potential for new insights.

Instruction

My working title is: "Comparison of the financial performance of companies with and without green bonds in the USA since 2020."

Analyze the entered topic and structure your feedback in three sections:

1. Suitability of the topic (brief assessment of whether the topic is fundamentally suitable)
2. Possible risks & pitfalls (critical aspects that could jeopardize success)
3. Suggestions for improvement (concrete ideas for refining or adjusting the topic)

Please consider the FINER criteria in each section:

- Feasible—Is the topic achievable within the available time and resources?
- Interesting—Is it of interest to the academic and, if applicable, practical community?
- Novel—Is new insight or an original contribution to be expected?
- Ethical—Are there ethical concerns or is the project justifiable?
- Relevant—Does it help answer a relevant question (e.g., societal, business-related, political)?

If individual aspects are unclear or information is missing, please formulate targeted follow-up questions or suggestions for self-clarification, rather than speculating on an uncertain basis.

Specifications

- Use a clear section structure with subheadings and numbering.
- If necessary, use bullet points or short paragraphs to present sub-aspects clearly.
- Explicitly refer to individual FINER criteria in your argumentation.
- Keep your language academic, advisory, and student-friendly.

5.3 Research Question and Choice of Methods

Formulating the research question is a significant step in planning a scientific paper and forms the starting point of every research project. A clearly defined and precise research question has a guiding function. It significantly influences the selection of literature, decisions about research design, and the methodology used to answer the question—so the extra time spent searching for the right research question is a worthwhile investment for students (Bryman, 2007; Nyiri, 2021). Thus, it lays the foundation for a structured and goal-oriented approach and is therefore also crucial for the success of the entire project.

A good research question fulfills several criteria (Kindler et al., 2019, p. 8): First, the question must be academically relevant, i.e., it must make a clear contribution to the chosen subject area. A well-considered research question usually consists of a main question, which forms the core of the investigation, and, if necessary, supplementary sub-questions that further deepen specific aspects. The formulation of the research question should be concise and precise to avoid misunderstandings and clearly define the focus. Another important characteristic is that the research question enables discussion and argumentation about the research subject and thus lays the foundation for a well-founded examination. In addition, the question must be designed so that it can be answered within the required or permissible length of the paper. A good research question also allows for a conclusion. That is, it should not only lead to the collection of information, but also allow for a final evaluation or answer. Finally, it is advisable to sharpen the research question according to personal interest in order to foster one's own engagement and motivation during the process.

AI can help in developing a research question or several research questions, structuring the topic, identifying key aspects, and formulating precise questions. Through targeted prompting—as in Prompt 5.6—narrowing questions can be generated to develop well-founded research questions with clear academic relevance and practical feasibility.

Prompt 5.6: Developing Research Questions for a Topic

Context

You are an experienced research advisor with expertise in supervising theses. You have a special talent for translating complex ideas into precise, actionable research questions. Your approach combines creativity with methodological rigor—always with a focus on academic relevance, clarity, potential for discussion, and feasibility.

Instruction

Step 1—Ask for the topic

Ask the user to name a research topic.

Step 2—Develop narrowing questions

Dynamically formulate five questions that help narrow the given topic down to a feasible research question.

Orient yourself to these criteria:

- Academic relevance
- Precision and delimitation
- Potential for discussion
- Feasibility (data, methods, time)
- Possibility for conclusion

Wait for the user's answers.
Step 3—Draft ideas for research questions
Based on the answers, create five research questions, each with up to three sub-questions and a brief justification of how the criteria are met.

Specifications

- Clearly and sequentially number all work steps (1–3).
- Use bullet points for sub-questions and justifications for readability.
- Keep the language clear and student-oriented, without resorting to technical jargon.

The prompt initiates a structured process that develops a precise and well-founded research question from a thematic idea. The AI assumes the persona of an experienced research advisor with the corresponding expertise and empathy. The process begins with clarifying the topic, followed by narrowing questions that help sharpen the focus and identify key aspects. The AI then develops concrete research questions with sub-questions that take into account both academic relevance and practical feasibility. This results in a question that is not only theoretically sound but also practically researchable.

In addition to developing new research questions, AI can also help revise and refine already formulated questions. It can check questions for clarity, precision, and academic relevance, point out unclear or overly broad formulations, and suggest alternative versions. It can also evaluate the logical structure and feasibility of the question and ensure that it meets academic standards.

Furthermore, AI can help further differentiate a research question by developing suitable sub-questions. These can illuminate various aspects of the main question, introduce methodological considerations, or provide a structure for later analysis. This is especially helpful when a question seems too general or it is not yet clear which perspectives are particularly relevant for the investigation. In this way, AI helps ensure that the research question is not only theoretically sound but also practically feasible.

Once a final research question has been formulated, AI can help develop and select an appropriate methodology. With a targeted prompt, various methodological approaches can be analyzed and their suitability for the specific question assessed. This is especially important because the chosen method not only determines the course and quality of the investigation but also influences the assessment of performance in academic work. A prompt can, for example, provide suggestions for qualitative or quantitative methods, point out suitable data collection and analysis techniques, or identify methodological challenges early on. Prompt 5.7 presents sample instructions to support students in selecting and justifying their methodology. This ensures that the method fits both the research question and the available resources and time constraints. If it turns out that a particular methodology is not practical or effective, it may be advisable to adjust the research question accordingly to ensure a well-founded and feasible study.

Prompt 5.7: Developing Methodology Based on the Research Question

Context

{*see Prompt 5.6*}

Instruction

Step 1—Research question
Ask me for my preferred or planned research question.
Step 2—List of research methods
Then create a tabular overview of the research methods suitable for this question. Add to the table the specific advantages and disadvantages of each method with regard to my research question.
Step 3—Recommendation
Give a clear recommendation for a methodology, with a brief justification of why it best fits the question. The methodology may include one or more combined methods (mixed methods).

Bonus: Also give me detailed tips and tricks, useful software tools, and possible pitfalls.

Specifications

- Present the overview in tabular form.
- Keep the table concise and user-friendly.
- Present your recommendation separately afterwards.

5.4 Pitfalls in Concept Development with AI

Despite the many advantages, the use of AI assistance should be approached with care. A central problem is the lack of transparency in many AI models, as students often cannot fully understand how the generated suggestions are produced. This creates the risk of uncritically adopting recommendations without questioning their content, or overlooking relevant topics and questions. It is therefore essential to critically examine the research questions proposed by AI: Do they really fit the topic? Are they precise enough? Do they align with your own academic considerations and goals?

Another risk is that the AI-supported process may tempt students to neglect intensive engagement with the academic literature. However, connecting one's own work with existing research is a central element of academic work and cannot be replaced. Literature serves not only as a source of information but also as a means of actively reflecting on the current state of knowledge and situating it within one's own argumentation.

Excessive dependence on AI can also weaken one's own critical thinking. If AI-generated suggestions are adopted without scrutiny, reflection and analytical engagement may take a back seat. Especially when developing a research question, it is crucial to understand the academic context and actively contribute your own ideas. AI can provide valuable impulses, highlight new perspectives, and help refine details. Nevertheless, academic work remains an independent intellectual achievement, in which students must take responsibility for their own decisions and consciously make key substantive choices.

In summary, a conscious and reflective approach to AI helps to leverage its strengths without neglecting core academic competencies.

5.5 Finding a Supervisor

Once the topic of the academic paper has been defined and an initial research question formulated, the inevitable next step is to find a suitable supervisor. Ideally, the search for a supervisor should not begin only after the exposé has been fully developed, but rather as soon as the first concrete idea for a topic emerges. This allows for a constructive dialogue to develop early on, in which expectations can be clarified, content priorities aligned, and the direction of the work jointly adjusted. Early agreement on goals, working methods, and communication culture forms the foundation for successful supervision. A shared understanding on both sides regarding the nature and scope of the collaboration significantly increases satisfaction with the supervisory relationship. This has been shown to have a positive effect on the progress and success of the thesis (Pyhältö et al., 2015).

Students associate good supervision with various expectations, some of which are particularly central (Doğan & Bıkmaz, 2015): They desire reliable and committed guidance, where agreements are honored and the supervisor remains accessible. At the same time, it is important to them that they are allowed to contribute and develop their own ideas without having their intellectual freedom restricted. Equally important are an encouraging tone and timely feedback on questions.

However, supervisors also have clear expectations of students. Supervisors emphasize the importance of initiative and independent problem-solving. Those who come well-prepared to meetings, bring concrete questions, and actively engage with and implement feedback not only demonstrate commitment but also facilitate collaboration and make targeted guidance possible in the first place (Lindgreen et al., 2002).

The choice of a suitable supervisor depends largely on the topic of the thesis and the planned methodological approach. For example, someone wishing to research process automation will hardly find the necessary subject-matter support from a chair specializing in leadership psychology. Similarly, a qualitative interview study is generally not well placed with a statistics professor whose focus is strongly quantitative. It is therefore crucial that the supervisor's content focus and methodological profile align well with your own project.

A sensible step in the search for a suitable supervisor is to systematically engage with your own topic of interest. You should check which professors or academic staff are working on related questions. Clues can be found in current publications, thematically relevant courses, or research projects. Looking at the faculty's website and having targeted conversations in seminars or with fellow students can also help identify suitable contacts.

It is helpful to compare your own topic with the publications of potential supervisors. This allows you to assess early on whether there are content-related points of connection. AI tools can support this comparison—for example, by analyzing publication lists and providing indications of thematic and methodological overlaps. An example of a suitable prompt can be found in Prompt 5.8.

Prompt 5.8: Checking Subject-Matter and Methodological Fit of a Supervisor

Context

You are an experienced academic advisor who has already successfully guided numerous students in choosing a suitable supervisor for their thesis. Your goal is to provide me with a well-founded assessment of whether a particular professor is suitable for my bachelor's thesis topic based on their thematic focus and methodological expertise.

Instruction

I am planning my bachelor's thesis on the topic [Topic]. Methodologically, I will likely be working with [Research Method].

Please use the following publication list to assess to what extent the professor's research interests and methodological orientation match my project. If possible, research additional information or abstracts for individual publications to substantiate your assessment.

Please address the following points:

1. Provide an overall overview of the extent to which there are thematic and methodological overlaps with my project.
2. Name and explain specific works that are particularly relevant to my topic or method.
3. Provide a final assessment of whether the professor appears suitable as a supervisor for my bachelor's thesis, with justification.

Requirements

- Use clear and comprehensible language appropriate for an academic advising context.
- Structure your response (e.g., with numbered sections or subheadings).
- Clearly present both matches and possible limitations.
- Clearly indicate and correctly attribute any researched information (e.g., abstracts).
- The assessment should provide a well-founded basis for deciding on a supervisor.

In the prompt, the AI is to take on the role of an academic advisor, comparing the topic and methodology with a publication list. In this example, only a general topic and a basic methodology are given. Alternatively, you can provide the provisional working title, central research questions, and the exact planned methodological approach in more detail.

Depending on the technical interface of the AI system used, publication lists can be integrated in various ways, such as by directly pasting them into the input field, uploading them as a text file, or providing a link to an online source. However, not every system is capable of automatically retrieving external information.

The main task in the prompt is to assess the thematic and methodological fit between your own project and the publication or research activities of the potential supervisor. In the first step, the AI creates an overall overview based on all available publications and derives general points of connection. In the second step, individual publications or projects that are particularly relevant to your own project are highlighted. These can then be specifically referenced in later contact—for example, in an email or conversation. Finally, the AI provides a summary assessment of the subject-matter and methodological fit.

It is important to emphasize that this analysis only covers the content level. For a successful supervisory relationship, personal factors such as communication compatibility, individual working style, or the supervisor's level of engagement also play a crucial role. Some instructors are more approachable, open, or structured than others. Those who immediately find common ground and a shared language often benefit from a trusting collaboration. Practical aspects such as workload and availability should also be considered. Especially with popular or highly engaged supervisors, it is advisable to make contact early and keep additional options open.

Finally, the choice of a second supervisor should not be neglected. It is advisable to select someone who complements the primary supervisor either in terms of content or methodology. Alternatively, a supervisor from industry or practice can be a good choice—for example, to bring in an application-oriented perspective or to emphasize the transfer to professional reality. This way, the thesis can be anchored not only in solid content but also in practical relevance (Spillner, 2023).

5.6 Creating an Outline

The outline forms the structural framework of an academic paper. It gives order to the argumentation and makes the thread of reasoning comprehensible to readers. Without a clear outline, content can easily become disconnected and central arguments lose their impact. A well-thought-out outline not only supports later readability but also helps guide you during the planning and research phase. It helps focus your literature review and set meaningful thematic priorities. Therefore, a preliminary outline should be created as early as possible, which can then be gradually developed and refined over the course of the work process (Oehlrich, 2014).

When developing the outline, some basic principles should be observed. First, the chosen principle of organization should be applied consistently across all levels. Switching the organizing principle within the paper can easily lead to ambiguities in the argumentation and make understanding more difficult. In addition, the outline should be balanced, meaning that the subpoints of a section should be roughly equally weighted and comparable in content. As a formal rule, a section should only be subdivided if it contains at least two subpoints. Conversely, there should not be more than about eight subpoints per outline level, as clarity is otherwise lost (Franck, 2024).

A helpful image for the structure of an academic outline is the metaphor of a barbell. At the beginning, there is a broad thematic introduction in which the topic is placed in a broader context, relevance and objectives are presented, and key terms, theories, or the state of research are introduced. In the main section, the perspective gradually narrows until it focuses on the specific object of investigation—for example, in the form of an empirical study or a detailed case analysis. In the final section, the perspective broadens again to the general, and the results are contextualized, critically reflected upon, and placed in a larger context. This corresponds to the classic three-step model of academic work: context of discovery, context of justification, and context of application, as shown in Table 5.3 (Raithel, 2008).

Based on this logic, the next task is to develop a suitable outline for your own paper. It is advisable to start at the macro level—that is, to define the main chapters that establish the basic structure of the argument. Only in the next step are these main chapters further differentiated by appropriate subchapters, resulting

Table 5.3 Three levels of the classic procedural model

	Context of Discovery	Context of Justification	Context of Application
Description	Describes the reason and motivation for the research	Encompasses all steps leading to the methodological processing and solution of the problem	Deals with the impact and implications of the research results
Questions	How did the idea arise? Why is it relevant? What is the situation?	What is the approach? Which methods, theories, hypotheses are applied?	For what are the results relevant? How can they be further used?
Typical Outline	Introduction, State of Research, Problem Statement	Methodology, Analysis, Results, Discussion	Implications, Conclusion, Outlook

in a clearly structured, hierarchically organized outline. Prompt 5.9 provides an example of how an AI chatbot can support this process through an interactive, step-by-step approach.

Prompt 5.9: Creating an Outline in Dialogue

Context

Please act as an academic advisor for academic writing. You possess in-depth subject knowledge, high methodological competence, and many years of advisory experience. Your role is to guide me in a structured, critical-constructive, and interactive manner in developing a purposeful and academically convincing outline for my academic paper.

Instruction

Work with me to develop the outline in an interactive three-step process. Only proceed to the next step once I have confirmed the previous one. My topic is [Topic] with the research question: [Research Question].

Step 1—Main Chapters
Ask me targeted questions about the topic, research question, method, and objectives of my paper. Based on this, suggest suitable main chapters and, if necessary, alternative structures. Ask follow-up questions if information is missing or unclear. Wait for my feedback before proceeding to step 2.
Step 2—Subchapters
For each main chapter I confirm:
Suggest suitable subchapters and divide them into mandatory subchapters (should be included) and optional subchapters (can be added).
Ask for my feedback before moving on to the next main chapter.
Step 3—Overall Check of the Outline

Check the completed outline for completeness, coherence, and goal orientation. Point out any missing or redundant parts and make concrete suggestions for improvement. Finally, provide a brief justification for why this outline is suitable for answering my research question.

Specifications

- Use clear chapter numbering (e.g., 1., 1.1, 1.2). In step 3, provide a correctly numbered outline (with no gaps in the numbering).
- Ensure that each main chapter contains at least two subchapters (or is intentionally left without subdivision).
- Write in simple, clear, and academically neutral language.
- If uncertain or information is missing, please ask targeted follow-up questions instead of making assumptions.
- Ensure that the outline is logically aligned with the research question and objectives.

In the underlying prompt, the AI takes on the role of an academic advisor who critically and constructively guides the structuring process. The goal is to develop a coherent outline in an interactive, multi-stage process that is both convincing in content and methodologically consistent.

The process begins with the development of the main chapters. Based on the topic, research question, and other information, the AI suggests various structural options, asks clarifying questions, and offers the opportunity to provide your own instructions. Only when the main structure has been approved by the user does the AI move on to the next step.

In the second step, suitable subchapters are proposed for each main chapter, step by step. The AI explains which elements are essential and which can be considered optional—depending on research design, scope, or focus. In this way, the entire outline is systematically built up, chapter by chapter.

Once the complete outline is in place and has also been approved, the AI conducts a final review. It provides suggestions for improvement and offers an overall assessment of the coherence, balance, and subject-matter consistency of the structure.

This dialogical and adaptive approach makes it possible to develop a robust outline step by step—always accompanied by explanations and opportunities for reflection. However, it is crucial not to blindly rely on the AI's suggestions. Instead, you should actively engage, ask questions, and understand the reasoning behind the structural proposals. Only those who fully grasp the logical structure of their own outline will later be able to convincingly fill it with content. A clear, well-thought-out outline is not only a helpful working tool but also an expression of academic judgment and thus a central quality feature of any academic paper.

An alternative approach is presented in Sect. 7.2, focusing on a deeper understanding of the functions of individual chapters and the relative distribution of the text.

5.7 Defining a Work Plan

The work or time plan for an academic paper specifies which steps are necessary in which chronological order to implement the planned project in a structured and timely manner. It translates the content design of the paper into concrete actions, thereby creating commitment in the work process. A key advantage of this type of planning is that it prompts you to systematically engage with the topic again and identify potential challenges early on. This makes it possible to schedule realistic time frames for labor-intensive phases such as literature research, data collection, or analysis, while also allowing for buffer times to accommodate unforeseen delays. In addition, a well-structured plan serves as a guide throughout the work process: it makes progress visible, enables self-monitoring, and can be motivating through intermediate goals—especially during longer, more complex writing phases (Folz, 2020).

To create a reliable work plan, the entire project must first be broken down into individual, clearly defined work steps. For each of these steps, you then need to estimate how much time should realistically be allocated. It is important to note that not all steps can be carried out independently of one another. There are often so-called path dependencies; for example, analysis can only begin once data collection is complete. For a viable plan, it is therefore essential to recognize these dependencies and take them into account in the sequence of work steps.

It is equally important to clarify the required resources early on. These include, for example, software for data analysis, specific materials, or external contacts. Those who clarify in advance when which resources will be needed can avoid bottlenecks and ensure that everything is available at the crucial moment.

Despite careful planning, one thing is inevitable: changes to the plan. Work steps often take longer than expected, unexpected problems force repetition of certain phases, or it becomes apparent that additional steps are required that were not previously considered. This phenomenon is so widespread that it has been humorously enshrined in what is known as Hofstadter's Law: "It always takes longer than you expect, even when you take into account Hofstadter's law." (Hofstadter, 1999)

The difficulties of realistic time planning are particularly evident in an experiment with students: In a seminar, participants were first asked how many days they thought they would need to complete their term paper. On average, the answer was about 34 days. They were then asked how long it would take in the best-case scenario—i.e., if everything went optimally without disruptions. Here, the average dropped to about 27 days. In the most pessimistic scenario, that is, if many things went wrong, they expected to need just under 49 days on average. After the seminar, it was checked how long the students had actually taken. The result was clear:

on average, they took over 55 days—not only far above their original estimate, but even well above their own assumed "worst case." In project management, this is also known as the planning fallacy (Buehler et al., 1994).

Given the risks and systematic misjudgments described, sound planning with ongoing self-monitoring is of central importance. AI can play a supportive role by helping to realistically estimate individual work steps, identify typical pitfalls early, and make potential risks visible. This not only allows for better time planning, but also for more proactive consideration of dependencies and bottlenecks. An example prompt showing how AI can provide this planning support can be found in Prompt 5.10.

Prompt 5.10: Designing a Project Plan

Context

You are an experienced academic project manager with numerous successfully completed projects. You plan accurately, risk-averse, and with attention to detail. Your task is to support me in creating a realistic, robust, and academically sound schedule for my thesis—including a milestone plan.

Instruction

I have a total of [Number] weeks to complete my academic paper. Please help me create a structured project plan with the following elements:

1. Breakdown: Break down the work based on my outline into work packages as well as the associated activities and milestones.
2. Dependencies: Show the dependencies between activities (what builds on what?).
3. Resources: Specify the resources required for each activity (e.g., software, lab, interview partners, etc.).
4. Time: Estimate the duration of each activity realistically (use time intervals, e.g., 1–2 weeks).
5. Overall Plan: Create an overall plan that takes logical path dependencies into account, includes realistic buffer times, and identifies possible parallelization of tasks.
6. Identify potential risks or bottlenecks (e.g., availability of interview partners, dependence on software access, etc.) in the plan and suggest concrete measures to minimize risks.

Specifications

- Present the plan as a structured table or Gantt chart with a timeline.
- Provide a one-sentence justification for each recommendation so I can understand and adapt the plan.
- Clearly highlight critical paths, risks, and bottlenecks (e.g., by using bold, symbols, or color coding).

- The plan should be realistic, robust, and feasible; avoid idealized assumptions.
- Use clear, precise language—the plan should also be suitable for communication with supervisors.

Once the role of an academic project manager has been defined, the actual structuring of the project begins with the help of AI. The entire academic paper is broken down into individual, manageable work packages. At this level of detail, dependencies can be identified: Which steps must be completed before others can begin? At the same time, the resources required for each step are recorded, such as software, access to literature, external contacts, or specific work materials.

A time interval is then estimated for each activity. The AI can assist by making its own estimates and discussing the plausibility of individual assessments with the user. Depending on the assessment, it can then be decided whether the average, the upper, or the lower end of the interval should be used as a reference value for further planning, depending on whether you want to plan more conservatively or optimistically.

Based on this groundwork, an overall plan can be developed that particularly takes into account path dependencies and necessary buffer times. This results in the so-called critical path: a chain of activities where any delay directly affects the entire schedule and thus the submission date. To be able to respond to unforeseen events, it is therefore advisable to plan generous time reserves at these points.

In this planning process, the AI can not only help identify the critical path, but also systematically analyze potential risks and bottlenecks and suggest appropriate countermeasures. For example, in empirical studies, the AI can point out the risk of a low response rate—a frequently underestimated risk in surveys or interview studies. Building on this, it offers concrete recommendations for action, such as using multiple recruitment channels or strategically over-recruiting by about 20% to compensate for dropouts. This guidance makes the planning more robust and, as a result, more realistic.

Finally, the AI visualizes the developed overall plan—depending on preference—in the form of a clear table or a Gantt chart. The latter is a proven project management tool that graphically displays timelines, dependencies, and the duration of individual work steps. An example of an AI-generated Gantt chart is shown in Fig. 5.3.

Despite its helpful functions, AI ultimately remains an advisory system based on probabilities and patterns—not on personal experience or human-like subject-matter understanding. AI recommendations can be inaccurate, incomplete, or, in individual cases, fundamentally wrong. Especially when it comes to time planning or assessing methodological risks, critical thinking is essential. Responsibility for the plan always remains with the author of the paper. Therefore, any plan created by AI should be carefully reviewed and ideally discussed with the supervisor. Comparing it with experience, institutional requirements, and realistic assessments

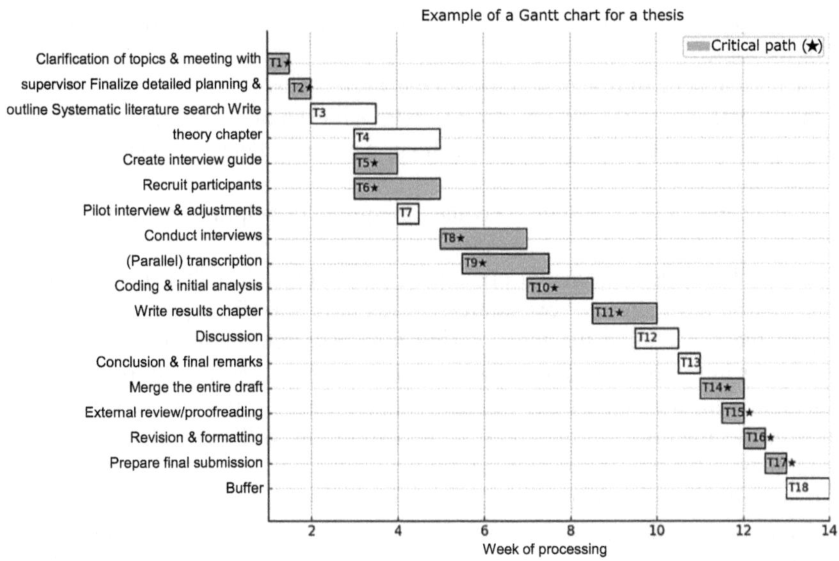

Fig. 5.3 Schedule as AI-generated gantt chart

is indispensable to avoid misjudgments and to put the plan on a solid foundation. For this reason, the work and time plan is also a fixed component of the exposé, which will be explained in more detail in the next subsection.

5.8 Writing an Exposé or Proposal

To make a good impression when requesting supervision, a meaningful exposé or proposal is always helpful. It outlines the planned project as a whole and provides a structured overview of the topic, research question, relevance, and methodological approach. Ideally, an exposé or proposal marks the conclusion of the planning phase. Precisely because the final result is often not yet foreseeable at this stage, thorough planning is all the more important—even if it seems demanding (Swoboda, 2023).

The aim of an exposé is to concisely present what the work is about, why the topic is relevant, and how it will be addressed. An exposé not only serves a communicative function, for example, to convince third parties such as potential supervisors. It also plays an important role for your own orientation: it helps clarify whether the topic has sufficient depth and whether you have already comprehensively understood and structured the subject matter.

An exposé should generally not exceed five to ten pages and typically contains the following components (Oehlrich, 2014):

- Topic and (provisional) working title;
- a rough outline of the planned chapters;

- the problem statement, which justifies the research rationale and the relevance of the topic;
- the current state of research on which the work is based;
- the objective of the work, i.e., what is to be achieved or answered;
- the planned methodological approach (in particular, details on data collection and analysis)
- if applicable, a work or time schedule, if required or helpful for structuring.

Based on the content discussed previously, it becomes clear that many elements of an exposé have already been addressed—as have specific applications of AI to support these. Defining the topic, formulating research questions, choosing the method, or initial considerations for the timeline can be specifically prepared and structured with the help of AI. Furthermore, AI can also provide valuable assistance in the linguistic formulation of the exposé, as will be explained in more detail in the following chapter ("Writing").

Especially when presenting the state of research, which must be done in a particularly condensed form in the exposé, AI can be used to summarize relevant literature or to shorten it selectively. The entire document can also be analyzed by AI in terms of structure, coherence, and readability. In such cases, the system takes on the role of a tutor, providing feedback on, for example, structure, consistency, and comprehensibility. An example of a suitable prompt can be found in Prompt 5.11.

Prompt 5.11: Revise Exposé

Context

You are an academic mentor who works with expertise, critical thinking, and empathy. Your task is to support me in creating a scientific exposé that not only convinces academically, but is specifically designed to win over a potential supervisor and make an excellent first impression.

Instruction

Please systematically analyze the exposé at hand based on the following five categories:

a. Clarity: Is the line of reasoning clear, precise, and comprehensible?
b. Linguistic Precision: Where can the expression be sharpened or the flow of reading improved?
c. Academic Style: Is appropriate and correct technical language used?
d. Coherence: Are the transitions and connections between sections logical and consistent?
e. Logic: Is the argumentation consistent, plausible, and convincingly structured?

For each of these five categories, provide:

1. Assessment: A brief qualitative evaluation of the respective category.
2. Weaknesses: A list of identified ambiguities, breaks, or inconsistencies.
3. Suggestions for improvement: Concrete, actionable recommendations for optimization.

Specifications

- Provide clearly structured feedback, ideally in the format:
  Category: Assessment, Weaknesses, Suggestions for improvement.
- Formulate your feedback in a goal-oriented, constructive, and comprehensible manner—no vague statements.
- Use respectful but honest language; mention strengths, but do not conceal weaknesses.
- If necessary, provide concrete text suggestions or alternative formulations, but without dominating my style.
- Do not just give correction hints, but justify your suggestions in a comprehensible way so that I understand the scientific principles behind them.

The particular strength of this prompt example lies in its clear, differentiated structure, which enables comprehensive yet targeted feedback. By dividing it into five defined categories (clarity, linguistic precision, academic style, coherence, and logical consistency), both formal and content-related aspects of an exposé are addressed. The structure also offers the necessary flexibility to delve deeper into individual categories as needed or to focus specifically on certain areas.

A key feature of the prompt is that the feedback is not merely superficial, but includes qualitative assessments, identification of weaknesses, and concrete suggestions for improvement. This threefold approach in particular helps make the learning process transparent and comprehensible for students. The requirements for justifying the feedback are of particular importance: they demand scientifically sound reflection from the AI, so that users can understand the logic of the argumentation and the underlying principles. This not only promotes understanding of the weaknesses in one's own text, but also imparts deeper knowledge of academic standards and their practical application. Another added value is that the prompt deliberately calls for open, honest, and constructive feedback. Large language models sometimes tend to sugarcoat statements or focus too much on being agreeable.

In conclusion, it can be stated that AI-based systems can substantially support the work process in creating an exposé and significantly improve the quality of the result. Nevertheless, it should be emphasized that the exposé should not be seen solely as a final product, but especially as a tool for reflection. For many supervisors, the main focus is that students engage intensively, comprehensively, and in a structured manner with the chosen topic. The goal is to prevent superficial or insufficiently thought-out approaches and instead to promote a holistic, well-founded problem analysis. For this reason, it is advisable to begin the exposé as much as possible without AI and to engage independently with the central questions. Only in a second step should AI tools be used more intensively to improve your own concept both in content and form. In this way, the exposé remains an authentic testimony to your individual engagement with the topic and, with AI support, its quality and excellence are further enhanced in the end.

5.9 Do's and Don'ts

Do's

1. *AI as an idea generator*: Start with brainstorming prompts to quickly generate variants, and refine them iteratively through follow-up questions and your own input.
2. *Activate tutoring mode*: Let the AI take on an empathetic advisory role, first asking smart questions and only then providing suggestions.
3. *Trend scouting*: Use AI on industry reports, conference proceedings, and theses to identify research gaps based on data.
4. *Narrowing down*: Use AI assistance for one or more delimitations to bring the topic to the right level of abstraction.
5. *Method selection*: Have the AI list the pros and cons of suitable methods in a table and address uncertainties through targeted follow-up questions.
6. *Outline co-creation*: Develop the chapter structure dialogically, but check consistency yourself.
7. *Timeline*: Use AI to draft a work and time schedule and have it highlight the critical path.
8. *Have exposé critiqued*: Ask the AI for structured feedback on clarity, style, coherence, logic, and specifically adapt text and structure.

Don'ts

1. *Copy & paste from AI*: Do not adopt unchecked text blocks or outlines due to the risk of hallucinations and plagiarism.
2. *One-prompt illusion*: A single prompt rarely suffices to generate a mature topic; iterative improvement is required.
3. *Shortcutting the literature*: Do not replace your own reading with pure AI summaries; otherwise, context and depth will be lacking.
4. *Method mismatch*: Avoid relying on smart AI method suggestions if the necessary resources or skills are lacking.
5. *Timeline without buffer*: Do not trust any overly optimistic AI planning that does not include buffers.
6. *Autopilot mode*: Do not hand over decision-making authority on topic, question, or conclusion to the AI—maintain critical thinking.

References

Bryman, A. (2007). The research question in social research: What is its role? *International Journal of Social Research Methodology, 10*(1), 5–20. https://doi.org/10.1080/13645570600655282.

Buehler, R., Griffin, D., & Ross, M. (1994). Exploring the „planning fallacy": Why people underestimate their task completion times. *Journal of Personality and Social Psychology, 67*(3), 366–381. https://doi.org/10.1037/0022-3514.67.3.366.

Cummings, S. R., Browner, W. S., & Hulley, S. B. (2013). Conceiving the research question and developing the study plan. In S. B. Hulley, S. R. Cummings, W. S. Browner, D. Grady, & T. B. Newman (Eds.), *Gale eBooks. Designing clinical research* (4. ed., pp. 14–22). Wolters Kluwer Health / Lippincott Williams & Wilkins.

Doğan, N., & Bıkmaz, Ö. (2015). Expectation of students from their thesis supervisor. *Procedia—Social and Behavioral Sciences, 174*, 3730–3737. https://doi.org/10.1016/j.sbspro.2015.01.1106.

Folz, K. (2020). *Zeitmanagement bei der Abschlussarbeit: Perfektes Timing für die Bachelor- und Masterthesis. Essentials*. Springer Gabler. https://doi.org/10.1007/978-3-658-28980-5.

Franck, N. (2017). *Handbuch wissenschaftliches Arbeiten: Was man für ein erfolgreiches Studium wissen und können muss* (3rd ed.). *UTB Schlüsselkompetenzen: Vol. 4748*. Verlag Ferdinand Schöningh. https://doi.org/10.36198/9783838547480.

Franck, N. (2024). *Schreiben im Studium: Wie Hausarbeiten und andere Texte gelingen: kompakte Antworten auf die 22 wichtigsten Fragen*. Springer VS. https://doi.org/10.1007/978-3-658-45377-0.

Goldenstein, J., Hunoldt, M., & Walgenbach, P. (2018). *Wissenschaftliche(s) Arbeiten in den Wirtschaftswissenschaften. Springer Fachmedien Wiesbaden*. https://doi.org/10.1007/978-3-658-20345-0.

Hofstadter, D. R. (1999). *Gödel, Escher, Bach: An Eternal Golden Braid* (20th anniversary ed.). Basic Books.

Kindler, H., Weber, F., Kühne, O., & Halder, G. (2019). *Wissenschaftlich arbeiten in Geographie und Raumwissenschaften: Ein Überblick. Essentials*. Springer VS. https://doi.org/10.1007/978-3-658-25631-9.

Kollmann, T., Kuckertz, A., & Stöckmann, C. (2016). *Das 1 x 1 des Wissenschaftlichen Arbeitens*. Springer Fachmedien. https://doi.org/10.1007/978-3-658-10707-9.

Lindgreen, A., Palmer, R., Vanhamme, J., & Beverland, M. (2002). Finding and choosing a supervisor. *The Marketing Review 3*(2) 147–166. https://doi.org/10.1362/146934702763487243.

Nyiri, Z. (2021). Getting the basics right: finding the right research question. In J. L. Bernstein (Eds.), *Elgar guides to teaching. Teaching research methods in political science*. Edward Elgar Publishing. https://doi.org/10.4337/9781839101212.00010.

Oehlrich, M. (2014). *Wissenschaftliches Arbeiten und Schreiben: Schritt für Schritt zur Bachelor- und Master-Thesis in den Wirtschaftswissenschaften*. Springer. https://doi.org/10.1007/978-3-662-44099-5.

Oulasvirta, A., Hukkinen, J. P., & Schwartz, B. (2009). When more is less. In J. Allan, J. Aslam, M. Sanderson, C. Zhai, & J. Zobel (Eds.), *Proceedings of the 32nd international ACM SIGIR conference on research and development in information retrieval* (pp. 516–523). ACM. https://doi.org/10.1145/1571941.1572030.

Pfister, G. (2021). Wie finde ich ein Thema für meine Abschlussarbeit. *WiSt—Wirtschaftswissenschaftliches Studium, 50*(12), 59–62. https://doi.org/10.15358/0340-1650-2021-12-59.

Pyhältö, K., Vekkaila, J., & Keskinen, J. (2015). Fit matters in the supervisory relationship: doctoral students and supervisors perceptions about the supervisory activities. *Innovations in Education and Teaching International, 52*(1), 4–16. https://doi.org/10.1080/14703297.2014.981836.

Raithel, J. (2008). *Quantitative Forschung: Ein Praxiskurs* (2nd ed.). VS Verlag. https://doi.org/10.1007/978-3-531-91148-9.

Schwartz, B. (2016). *The paradox of choice: Why more is less* (Revised edition). ECCO Press.

Spillner, V. (2023). *Sprechstunde Bachelorarbeit und Masterarbeit: In 10 Schritten ohne Stress und Zweifel zum Erfolg bei wissenschaftlichen Arbeiten*. Springer. https://doi.org/10.1007/978-3-658-41431-3.

Swoboda, M. (2023). *Wissenschaftlich schreiben leicht gemacht: Ein Leitfaden für Architektur- und Designstudiengänge*. Springer Vieweg. https://doi.org/10.1007/978-3-658-42166-3.

Tepper, R. (2012, June 5th). *Subway boasts 37 million possible sandwich variations around the world*. HuffPost. https://www.huffpost.com/entry/subway-sandwiches-world_n_2023347.

Williams, H. K. (1919). Religious education: The group plan. In W. R. Harper, E. D. Burton, & S. Mathews (Eds.), *The biblical world* (pp. 80–81). University of Chicago Press.

6 Literature: AI in Literature Research

Abstract

This chapter addresses the transformation of scholarly literature review in the digital age and the role of artificial intelligence (AI) as a supportive tool. Starting from traditional literature research methods—keyword search, backward and forward search—it demonstrates how these can be expanded and systematized through AI. The focus is on the targeted development of search strategies, the evaluation of scholarly sources, and the structured understanding of key content. Concrete AI-based prompts are presented that generate search terms, check relevance criteria, analyze publications, and assist in note-taking. The chapter emphasizes the importance of critical reflection and the active role of researchers, as AI cannot fully perform content evaluations, theoretical contextualizations, or methodological analyses. Limitations such as restricted data access, potential misjudgments, and the risk of context-free interpretations are also discussed. Overall, the chapter provides practical insights into how the combination of human expertise and AI technology can enhance both the efficiency of literature review work and scientific quality.

"Reading is to the mind, what exercise is to the body."
– Joseph Addison (1709, p. 117)

6.1 The Role of Literature

Scientific literature forms the foundation for one's own academic work. By taking up, further developing, and critically reflecting on existing knowledge, researchers position themselves within the ongoing scientific discourse (Snyder, 2019). Isaac Newton already formulated this principle with the famous words: "If I have seen further it is by standing on the shoulders of giants" (quoted in Chen, 2003).

F. Lang, *Using Artificial Intelligence in Term Papers and Theses*,
https://doi.org/10.1007/978-3-662-73208-3_6

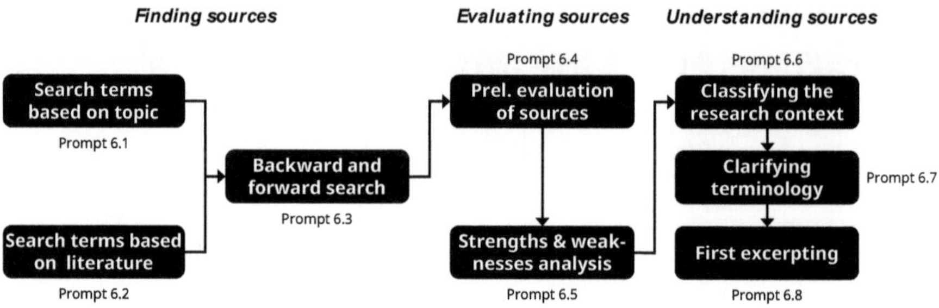

Fig. 6.1 Finding, evaluating, and understanding literature with AI

This quote illustrates that every new insight is built on the foundation of previous research—a thought so essential that the phrase "On the shoulders of giants" appears on the homepage of the scholarly search engine Google Scholar.

The way scientific literature is handled has fundamentally changed due to digitalization. Before the spread of the internet, long days in the library were a matter of course for students, and important findings were laboriously recorded by hand or with photocopies (Clarke, 1963). Access to specialist literature was limited to printed works in libraries, and research required a high degree of physical presence and organizational effort.

Whereas in the past the challenge was to gain access to relevant information at all, today the difficulty lies primarily in managing the enormous abundance of information. Scientific output has grown exponentially and doubles every 15–20 years (Bornmann et al., 2021). Access to publications is easier than ever thanks to digital search engines, online databases, and open-access platforms. However, this development brings a new problem: the available volume of scientific texts often exceeds the capacity to fully comprehend and systematically process them.

It is therefore more important than ever to approach literature research methodically and in a structured manner. Only through targeted selection of relevant sources, critical engagement with existing research findings, and thoughtful organization of one's own knowledge can scientific progress be meaningfully advanced. AI can support and facilitate this process, but it does not replace scientific reflection and evaluation by humans.

Figure 6.1 illustrates the various ways AI can be used throughout the entire literature research process. These range from identifying relevant sources and assessing their scientific quality to supporting content comprehension.

6.2 Finding Sources

Literature search is based on three central methods: keyword search, backward search, and forward search (see Fig. 6.2). The process begins with a keyword search, in which technical terms are entered into scholarly search engines such

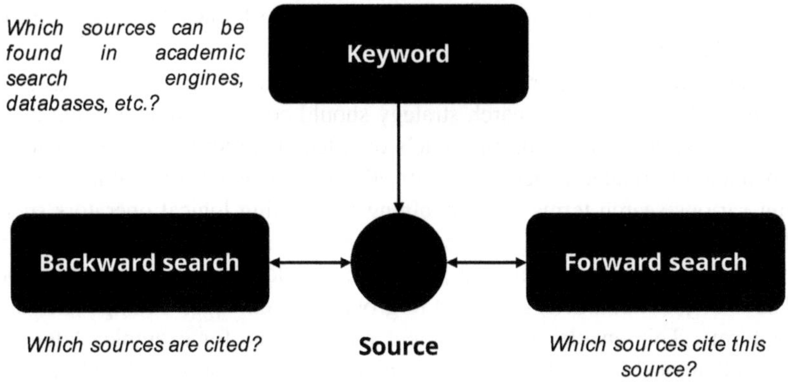

Fig. 6.2 Three types of literature search

as Google Scholar or Semantic Scholar, as well as subject-specific databases like Web of Science or Scopus, to identify relevant publications. Alternatively, the search can be conducted directly via publisher websites, academic journals, or library catalogs. The success of this method depends largely on the choice of precise and specific search terms.

Once a relevant source has been found, the next step is backward search. This involves analyzing the reference list of the publication to find out which works it cites. Since academic texts generally build on existing research, this method leads to older, often foundational studies in a research field. By systematically examining the cited works, key theories and concepts of a topic can be uncovered.

In addition, forward search enables the identification of more recent publications that cite an already identified source. This allows current developments and ongoing discussions in the research area to be captured. Scholarly search engines and databases such as Google Scholar or Web of Science offer functions that display all subsequent works referencing a particular source (Goldenstein et al., 2018).

The entire process of literature research is dynamic and iterative. Combining keyword search, backward, and forward search leads to a structured exploration of the state of research. The search ends when a comprehensive overview of the topic has been achieved and no new relevant citations can be identified (Schryen, 2015).

The choice of suitable keywords is crucial for the success of a literature search. In modern literature search systems, not only the explicitly stated keywords of a publication are searched, but also its title, abstract, and, if applicable, content, to identify relevant results. Many literature search systems also offer advanced search functions that allow queries to be refined in a targeted manner. These include, among others, filters by subject area, year of publication, or citation frequency, as well as the ability to use logical operators such as AND/OR and wildcards (e.g., *). By skillfully combining these techniques, search accuracy can be optimized and the research effort significantly reduced (Guba, 2008). In addition to inclusion criteria, exclusion criteria can also help to search the knowledge base more precisely (Fink, 2014).

AI can be used to support the development of suitable search terms, as shown in Prompt 6.1: An effective search strategy should cover as broad a range of keywords as possible, so that not only one's own technical terms but also synonyms and thematically related concepts are considered. This is where AI comes in, generating various search terms and combining them using logical operators such as AND or OR. This allows for more comprehensive and precise search queries that capture a larger number of relevant publications. Additionally, AI can incorporate wildcards or joker characters (e.g., *) to group different word endings and inflectional forms. This enables more efficient research, as, for example, "algorith*" will simultaneously include terms like "algorithm," "algorithms," and "algorithmic." Of course, the approach can be flexibly adapted to different search engines or databases and languages. It is necessary to observe the specific syntax rules of the platform used and, if necessary, include specific instructions in the prompt if the AI assistant does not recognize them independently.

Prompt 6.1: Automated Generation of Search Terms

Context

You are an experienced academic research expert with strong methodological competence in literature research. You support me in developing a systematic search strategy. The goal is to find high-quality academic publications in scholarly search engines such as Google Scholar that comprehensively cover my topic and research question.

Instruction

Formulate several precise search terms for a systematic search on Google Scholar that best cover my research topic and research question.

Please observe the following criteria:

- Use English terms only.
- Use Boolean operators (AND, OR, NOT, "…") and wildcard characters (e.g., *) to logically link terms and include variants.
- Ensure that the search terms cover a broad but still relevant spectrum of academic publications.
- Also identify terms that should be excluded from the search, if applicable.
- Formulate several search strings for different focuses or perspectives on the topic.

Specifications

- Organize the search terms thematically or functionally, e.g., by main term, method, application context, etc.
- Provide a brief explanation for each search string, indicating which aspect of the research question it covers.

- Ensure a clear, tabular, or structured presentation so that the search terms can be easily adapted or adopted.
- The language of the explanations should be clear, concise, and application-oriented—ideal for students.

The result of the prompt is a structured list of relevant search terms that enable comprehensive research with a scholarly search engine or database.

This approach is particularly helpful when the research topic is still unfamiliar and a broad search is therefore required. In some cases, however, it is possible to identify initial works early in the research process that are particularly relevant to one's own research question. Instead of continuing to search broadly, these initial findings can be used in a targeted manner to find further thematically appropriate sources. AI can assist here by analyzing the identified publications. For example, it can evaluate the bibliographic information (authors, year, journal) and the abstract to derive key search terms. These terms can then be used to specifically search for further publications that are similar in content or address related aspects of the research question. Prompt 6.2 demonstrates this approach by using already identified key sources to specifically identify search terms for further literature.

Prompt 6.2: Search Terms Based on Already Identified Literature

Context

{see Prompt 6.1}

Instruction

Based on the provided sources, create several precise search terms for a search in a scholarly search engine such as Google Scholar that identify thematically comparable or related sources to those provided.

Use the following to formulate:

- Boolean operators (AND, OR, NOT)
- Wildcard characters (*), where appropriate
- Technical terms, key concepts, theories, or methods used in the original sources

Specifications

{see Prompt 6.1}

After the search query has been executed, the sources found must be checked for their relevance to the research topic (see Sect. 6.3). This involves analyzing whether the identified publications are relevant to the research context and enable further engagement with the topic. The sources classified as thematically related and relevant provide starting points for further literature through forward and backward search: in backward search, the references cited in the found source's bibliography are examined. In forward search, on the other hand, it is analyzed which later publications cite the found source.

The lists resulting from forward and backward search contain numerous additional references. However, not all cited or citing works are relevant to one's own research topic, so a systematic selection is required. In practice, this preselection is usually made by initially screening the titles and abstracts of the listed publications. AI can assist here by pre-evaluating the suitability of sources, filtering by thematic matches, keywords, or methodological aspects.

Prompt 6.3 demonstrates how this can be implemented in practice, showing an AI-supported pre-selection of relevant literature from a forward or backward search. The sources are checked for their relevance to the research question. The works are categorized into three groups based on their content, methodological orientation, and findings: high relevance, medium relevance, or not relevant. Each classification is also accompanied by a brief justification to make the decision transparent and verifiable. In this process, AI serves only as a supporting tool, while the final evaluation of the literature always remains the responsibility of the researcher. This means that both sources classified as highly relevant and those classified as not relevant should be critically reviewed again. Especially for sources with medium relevance, a careful content analysis is required, as their usefulness for the research question is not immediately apparent. Thus, AI facilitates the preselection and structuring of literature but does not replace the well-founded assessment and expert evaluation by humans.

Prompt 6.3: Preliminary Review of a Literature List from Forward or Backward Search

Context

You are an experienced researcher with in-depth expertise in the analysis and preparation of academic literature as well as advanced knowledge in systematic literature analysis, meta-analysis, and reviews. You have a trained eye for the content, methodological, and empirical relevance of academic sources and support me in evaluating and classifying existing literature with regard to my research question.

Instruction

Systematically analyze the following literature list with regard to its content, methodological, and result-specific relevance to my research question. Clearly assign each source to one of the following three categories:

- *High relevance*: The source is highly likely to contribute directly to answering the research question.

- *Medium relevance*: The source contains potentially useful information, but its relation to the research question is not clear or is indirect.
- *No relevance*: The source obviously offers no content, methodological, or theoretical connection to the research question.

Provide a brief, comprehensible justification for each classification.

If a source is difficult to assess, state the reason for the uncertainty (e.g., unclear title, missing abstract) and describe how you dealt with it (e.g., brief research, provisional assessment with reservation).

Specifications

- Include all sources in the literature list—no omissions, do not stop until all entries have been processed.
- At the end, provide a clear summary, e.g., as a numbered list or table:

a) Title
b) Classification (high/medium/no relevance)
c) Justification

- Also provide a brief overall summary: How many titles fall into each relevance category?
- Use clear, academically objective language—no evaluations of the author or style, focus only on content relevance to the research question.
- The classification should serve as a basis for a later systematic literature analysis or review.

6.3 Evaluating Sources

The identified sources must now be assessed for their suitability for your own academic work. For a source to be included in an academic paper, three central criteria must be met (Prexl, 2019):

1. Citeability
2. Worthiness of citation
3. Relevance

A source is **citable** if it is permanently and unrestrictedly accessible, so that readers can easily find it and independently verify the information provided. While publications available through bookstores, libraries, or permanent links such as those for digital journals are generally considered citable, this is often not the case for so-called "grey literature" such as unpublished theses, internal company documents, or confidential papers, as access to them may be restricted (Prexl, 2019).

To determine whether a source is **worthy of citation**, various requirements must be met: One is that it is written by trustworthy authors who ideally have academic qualifications in the relevant field. It is also crucial that the publication addresses a clearly formulated academic research question, follows a methodologically sound and structured approach, and supports its argumentation with precise academic language and references to relevant sources. Quality assurance is ideally provided by a recognized publication medium, such as a peer-reviewed journal (i.e., articles are reviewed by other scholars) or a reputable academic publisher that ensures content review by subject experts. If these features are missing, or if essential elements such as methodological foundation or references are absent, the worthiness of citation should be critically questioned (Kindler et al., 2019; Prexl, 2019).

Finally, a source is **relevant** if it has a direct content-related connection to your own research question and contributes to answering the research question. Current publications from reputable academic journals or by recognized scholars should be preferred, while older studies or contributions from practitioners and journalists should only be used as supplementary sources (Prexl, 2019).

These requirements for a source can be preliminarily checked using AI by integrating the identified reference—ideally supplemented by additional information such as the abstract or the full paper—into a prompt such as Prompt 6.4. Based on the given instructions, the AI analyzes the source in terms of citeability, worthiness of citation, and relevance, and presents the results in a structured overview. AI assistants with integrated web search are particularly suitable, as they can retrieve additional data from academic databases and develop a broader contextual understanding. However, the assessments generated by AI should always be interpreted with caution, as they can only serve as an initial indication. Important aspects such as verifying a peer-review process or the academic reputation of the authors may be incomplete or may be incorrectly represented or hallucinated by the AI. Therefore, the final evaluation of the source remains an academic task that must be supplemented by manual review and critical reflection by the author.

Prompt 6.4: Preliminary Assessment of the Academic Suitability of Sources

Context

{see, e.g., Prompt 6.3}

Instruction

Please assess the suitability of the following source according to the following three categories:

1. Citeability
   - Permanent and unrestricted accessibility:
     e.g., publication in bookstores, via libraries, or as a stable online source with DOI or institutional archiving

2. Worthiness of citation
   - Author and qualification:
     Does the author have academic qualifications and a reputation in the relevant field?
   - Academic research question and methodology:
     Is a clearly defined academic research question addressed with a comprehensible methodology?
   - Argumentation and sources:
     Is the argumentation precise, logical, and supported by sources (including references)?
   - Quality assurance:
     Was the source published in a recognized academic publication medium (e.g., peer-reviewed journal or reputable publisher)?
   - Conflicts of interest:
     Are there indications of possible bias or financial influence by external actors?
3. Relevance
   - Relation to the research question:
     Does the source have a clear content-related connection (theoretical, empirical, or methodological) to my research question?

Specifications

- Answer each point in a structured and precise manner, with a brief justification.
- At the end, provide an overall assessment of whether the source is fully, partially, or not citable.
- If necessary, try to research additional information on the internet.
- Please present the assessment in a table and highlight any concerns in bold. If an assessment in a criterion cannot be clearly made, please indicate this accordingly.

In addition to the fundamental question of whether a source is suitable for academic work at all, the quality of the source also plays a decisive role. While authors and the publication medium provide initial indications of academic quality, a content analysis of the text is required to make a well-founded assessment of its strengths and weaknesses. However, this evaluation is time-consuming and requires a detailed examination of the methodology, argumentation, and significance of the publication. The targeted use of AI can significantly facilitate this process by systematically checking key quality criteria and providing a structured initial assessment.

Prompt 6.5 shows how AI can be used for the preliminary assessment of academic texts. The prompt instructs the AI to analyze the text based on key academic quality criteria, including methodological foundation, representativeness of the sample, validity and reliability of the results, transparency of research documentation, and handling of limitations. An example of such an analysis would be the examination of an empirical study: the AI can check whether the data collection design is clearly described, whether the sample is large enough and methodologically appropriate, or whether the authors adequately reflect and transparently present possible weaknesses of the study.

The result of the prompt provides a structured assessment in tabular form, enabling an initial well-founded evaluation of the publication. This makes it easier to quickly identify which statements in a source should be read with caution and to what extent the results can provide a valuable addition to one's own work.

Prompt 6.5: Assessment of the Strengths and Weaknesses of a Publication

Context

{see, e.g., Prompt 6.3}

Instruction

Please assess the following academic text based on the methodological quality criteria listed below. Address strengths and weaknesses and consider the following questions:

- Well-founded and transparent methodology: Is the research design clearly described and logically justified?
- Appropriate and representative sample: Is the selection of participants methodologically appropriate and representative of the target population?
- High validity and reliability of results: Were valid measurement instruments used and is the reproducibility of the results ensured?
- Clear, comprehensible presentation of the procedure: Is the entire research process (data collection, analysis, etc.) coherently documented?
- Handling of limitations: Are the limitations of the study openly addressed? What restrictions exist, and how significantly do they affect the validity of the findings?

Afterwards, please provide a final overall assessment of whether the study—also taking possible shortcomings into account—can be considered a reliable academic source. Justify your assessment in a comprehensible manner.

Specifications

- Present your assessment in tabular form:
  Criterion | Strengths | Weaknesses.

- The overall assessment at the end should be clearly justified (1–2 paragraphs, below the table).
- Formulate objectively, analytically, and in a scientifically neutral manner—no sweeping judgments.

6.4 Understanding Sources

Thorough reading of scientific sources remains essential, but AI can facilitate the path to understanding by helping to structure key content, identify relationships, and prepare relevant information for later use. Especially in the early phase of literature research, AI can assist in quickly gaining an overview of a publication by systematically extracting essential aspects of the research context.

The research context includes, among other things, identifying the research question, methodology, and key findings that characterize a publication. While this information is often already included in the abstract, it may be abbreviated, incomplete, or formulated in complex technical language. With AI, such content can be processed and presented in a structured way, making it easier to initially classify the content.

Prompt 6.6 demonstrates how such AI-supported processing can be carried out. The prerequisite for this process is that the scientific text is either inserted directly into the prompt or provided as an attachment. Through this automated analysis, the reader receives a well-founded overview of the central content of the source and can focus specifically on the relevant passages of the text.

Once the research context has been clarified, the next step is to engage intensively with the text, especially with the theories, key terms, and concepts used within it. Placing the work within the theoretical or scientific knowledge base often requires further research, as key terms or theoretical models are not always explained in detail in the respective source, but must be inferred from other scientific publications in order to understand their precise meaning and application in the research context (Oehlrich, 2014).

Prompt 6.6: Processing the Research Context

Context

{see, e.g. Prompt 6.3}

Instruction

Please analyze the following scientific text and summarize the relevant content clearly under the following five points:

- Defining the thematic framework: Which key terms characterize the research topic and what exactly is being investigated?

- Research questions: What specific questions are addressed in the source?
- Embedding in existing theories and models: Which established theories, concepts, or models does the study draw upon?
- Capturing the methodological framework: Which methods or methodological approaches are used (e.g., qualitative, quantitative, mixed methods)?
- Key findings: What are the central results and findings of the study, and what conclusions are drawn from them?

Specifications

- Summarize all findings in a clearly structured table:
  Criterion | Content Summary | Remark (optional).
- Use precise, scientifically neutral language:

AI can specifically support this process by, for example, researching definitions for technical terms, concisely summarizing concepts, or illustrating their meaning with practical examples. Prompt 6.7 illustrates such an approach by starting from a list of technical terms, theories, or constructs that are to be further explained and placed in the scientific context. While it would be conceivable for AI to automatically extract all relevant key terms from the text, this presents two challenges: On the one hand, an information overload could occur, making the actual analysis more difficult, and on the other hand, critical review remains essential. Every explanation must be checked against one's own understanding or the source to identify possible misinterpretations.

Prompt 6.7: Clarification and Classification of Terminology

Context

{see, e.g. Prompt 6.3}

Instruction

Please analyze the following scientific text, taking into account the attached list of terms. For each term, you should provide the following four pieces of information:

- Definition: A clear, concise definition of the term in the specific context of the text
- Explanation: A brief explanation of the central features or theoretical significance of the term, as well as, if available, references to underlying theories, concepts, or models

- Practical example: A concrete application or scenario that makes the meaning of the term understandable
- Notes: Relevant sources or further literature for deeper study; if applicable, critical comments, open questions, or contradictions in the text associated with the term

Specifications

- Present the results in a clear table:
  Term | Definition | Explanation | Practical Example | Notes.
- For terms for which there is not enough information in the text, mark this clearly (e.g., "not fully derivable") and recommend suitable research strategies or literature sources for further clarification.
- Use clear, objective language—suitable for students engaging in in-depth study of the topic.
- The table should serve as a learning aid and analysis tool—compact, informative, and differentiated.

A proven method for the structured processing of scientific texts is excerpting. In this process, key statements from a text are extracted and systematically documented with regard to one's own research question. This can be done either by collecting literal quotations from the original text or by paraphrasing summaries that reproduce the core statements in one's own words. The goal of excerpting is to efficiently capture relevant information so that it can later be incorporated into one's own scientific argumentation (Beek et al., 2018; Franck, 2017; Kornmeier, 2024).

Prompt 6.8 shows how this process can be automatically supported with AI. The AI can provide an initial structural processing by identifying relevant passages and outputting them as excerpts. This makes the initial round of groundwork more efficient, which is especially beneficial for extensive texts and can save considerable time. Nevertheless, it is essential to critically review and revise the automatically generated excerpts. This not only ensures that all relevant statements have been correctly captured, but also helps to avoid errors or hallucinations that may arise from the AI. In addition, manual editing allows for more precise adaptation of the excerpts to one's own research focus and ensures that key concepts are correctly interpreted. Thus, AI can serve as a valuable support in the process, but it does not replace scientific reflection and evaluation by the researcher.

Prompt 6.8: Initial Excerpting with AI

Context

{see, e.g., Prompt 6.3}

Instruction

Please excerpt the following text specifically with regard to my research question. Identify the key statements that are substantively related to the question. For each statement, please use the following four-part structure:

1. Topic of the statement: Brief classification of the aspect addressed (e.g., theoretical framework, methodological approach, empirical finding)
2. Statement: Core statement in your own words, formulated precisely and concisely
3. Quotation (optional, if relevant): Literal quotation from the original text that illustrates the statement (possibly shortened, with quotation marks and page reference)
4. Comment/Relevance to my research question: Why is this statement significant for my research question? Are there any ambiguities or open points for discussion?

Specifications

- Present the excerpts in a structured table with the four columns from the structure above.
- Use clear, scientifically objective language.
- Select statements that are substantively robust and central to the research question—no marginal notes.

6.5 Challenges and Limitations

The use of AI can significantly facilitate literature research and analysis. However, the use of AI in this area is also associated with significant challenges and limitations that must be taken into account when using these technologies.

Limited Access to Scientific Literature A central problem of AI-supported literature research is that many scientific publications are protected behind paywalls or licensing systems and are therefore not freely accessible. As a result, AI models are often only able to retrieve metadata or abstracts, while the full text of the publication is not included in the analysis. Consequently, the research remains incomplete, as potentially relevant sources may be overlooked or only superficially evaluated. Related to this is the tendency of AI assistants to primarily rely on publicly available information, which can result in an overrepresentation of freely accessible but not necessarily high-quality scientific sources. This can lead to preprints, open-access publications, or non-peer-reviewed articles playing a larger role in the results than higher-quality, but licensed, scholarly articles.

It therefore remains essential to conduct the core research oneself and to specifically access licensed literature. Students should familiarize themselves with the access options at their institution, especially databases, digital library services, and interlibrary loan systems, in order to incorporate scientifically sound and peer-reviewed sources into their own work.

Limitations in the Evaluation of Scientific Sources AI may have difficulty accurately assessing the actual scientific relevance of a source. Especially when it comes to content evaluation, such as methodological suitability or theoretical foundation, misjudgments can occur—particularly if the AI does not clearly recognize discipline-specific paradigms or lacks domain-specific expertise. In many cases, AI relies on quantitative metrics such as citation frequency or the impact factor of a journal, which may indicate the visibility of a publication but do not necessarily reflect its substantive quality. These metrics can be misleading, as they often do not distinguish between positive reception and critical engagement.

Furthermore, there is a risk that AI accesses incomplete or incorrect metadata. For example, information about whether a publication has undergone peer review is not always clearly available and cannot be automatically verified. The same applies to contextual information such as the scientific reputation of the authors, their institutional affiliation, or any conflicts of interest. If such information is missing or inaccurate, the risk of hallucinations increases.

For these reasons, AI-supported source evaluation can only serve as an initial orientation by highlighting possible strengths or weaknesses of a source. The final assessment—whether a source is citable, worthy of citation, and relevant—remains the responsibility of the student, who must make a well-founded decision about the suitability of the source for their own work.

Errors or Misunderstandings in Text Comprehension Even when it comes to understanding scientific texts, AI can only provide support—working through, critically reflecting on, and contextualizing the literature remains a central task for the author. Scientific terms can be defined or connoted differently in various disciplines and theoretical contexts, making it difficult for AI to capture them accurately. Due to its technical functioning, AI struggles to distinguish between general and field-specific definitions. In some cases, colloquial meanings may even override more precise technical definitions, leading to misunderstandings. Furthermore, automatically generated summaries tend to remain superficial, which can result in missing key details and contextual backgrounds. This can distort the original meaning of the source or leave important findings unconsidered. Even if the AI is only supposed to extract information from a given source text, there is still a risk that content will be supplemented by hallucinations or misinterpreted.

Ultimately, literature review work is not just about compiling a complete collection of sources and excerpts, but rather about developing one's own understanding of the subject matter. Scientific work means not only grasping concepts and theories, but also questioning them, placing them in a broader context, and engaging with them critically. AI can serve as a tool to structure and facilitate the process, but it does not replace active and reflective engagement with scientific literature. The central goal remains to develop a deep understanding of the subject matter through one's own reading, analysis, and questioning, and thus to further one's scientific education.

Conclusion In summary, AI can significantly facilitate literature review work by optimizing search processes, structuring relevant sources, and creating concise summaries. This makes processing large amounts of information more efficient, allowing researchers to focus more specifically on content analysis. However, human expertise remains essential, especially for the critical evaluation, classification, and interpretation of scientific literature. While AI models support the collection and organization of information, they lack a deep understanding of scientific theories, methodological nuances, and discipline-specific paradigms. Only through personal reflection and analytical thinking can researchers make well-founded judgments about the quality, relevance, and significance of scientific findings.

The greatest added value arises from a combination of AI-supported techniques and human reflection, in which the researcher actively engages with the content, places it in the scientific context, and critically questions it. While AI can accelerate and structure the research process, the well-founded evaluation, classification, and interpretation of scientific sources remains an indispensable human task. The overarching goal of scientific work is not just to collect literature, but to understand it and integrate it into one's own work. This intellectual engagement can be supported by AI, but by no means replaced.

6.6 Do's and Don'ts

Do's

1. *Clearly assign responsibility*: AI serves as a supportive tool—responsibility for the selection, evaluation, and interpretation of scientific sources lies with the human user.
2. *Critical source review*: Consistently check every source for citability, worthiness of citation, and relevance before including it in your work.
3. *Transparent use of AI*: Clearly document methodology, tools, and prompts so that the research and analysis process remains traceable.
4. *Qualitative evaluation*: Have AI initially prepare a table of strengths and weaknesses (e.g., methodology, validity, limitations) of a publication and then review the results yourself.
5. *Contextual understanding*: AI can assist with summaries, clarifications of terms, and excerpts, but for a sound understanding, independent engagement with the original texts is indispensable.

6. *Maintain data protection*: When uploading unpublished data or full articles, pay attention to copyright and licensing rights as well as institutional guidelines.
7. *Focus efficiently*: Use AI primarily where it accelerates routine tasks (search, sorting, formatting), and invest the time saved in substantive depth.

Don'ts

1. *Blind trust*: Never adopt AI outputs without verification—hallucinations, outdated data, or misinterpretations are common.
2. *Unreflective citation*: Do not cite sources that have only been suggested by AI without having read them yourself.
3. *Relying solely on numbers*: Do not judge the quality of a study solely on the basis of citation counts, impact factor, or rankings provided by AI.
4. *Loss of context*: Summaries alone, such as from abstracts, are not sufficient, as key information on methodology, sample, or limitations may otherwise be overlooked.
5. *Over-automation*: Do not delegate all excerpting or analysis tasks to AI; your own contribution is required both in terms of content and examination regulations.
6. *Adopting hallucinations*: Avoid transferring AI chat responses directly into the bibliography; check authorship, year, and DOI manually.
7. *Losing source diversity*: AI often relies on freely available open-access sources, but balanced literature review work also requires the inclusion of licensed, high-quality scholarly publications.

References

Addison, J. (1709). *The Tatler, No 147. Saturday, March 18, 1709.* University of Michigan Library Digital Collections. In the digital collection Eighteenth Century Collections Online. https://name.umdl.umich.edu/004786805.0001.000.

Beek, M., Grzanna-Zschoke, C., Jäger, R., Kuhlenkasper, T., & Molitor, E. (2018). Literaturerschließung. In S. Stock, P. Schneider, E. Peper, & E. Molitor (Eds.), *Erfolgreich wissenschaftlich arbeiten* (pp. 69–77). Springer. https://doi.org/10.1007/978-3-662-55001-4_5.

Bornmann, L., Haunschild, R., & Mutz, R. (2021). Growth rates of modern science: A latent piecewise growth curve approach to model publication numbers from established and new literature databases. *Humanities and Social Sciences Communications, 8*(1). https://doi.org/10.1057/s41599-021-00903-w.

Chen, C. (2003). On the shoulders of giants. In C. Chen (Ed.), *Mapping scientific frontiers: The quest for knowledge visualization* (pp. 135–166). Springer. https://doi.org/10.1007/978-1-4471-0051-5_5.

Clarke, R. F. (1963). *The Impact of Photocopying on Scholarly Publishing*. Rutgers The State University of New Jersey, School of Graduate Studies.

Fink, A. (2014). *Conducting Research Literature Reviews: From the Internet to Paper* (4. ed.). SAGE.

Franck, N. (2017). *Handbuch wissenschaftliches Arbeiten: Was man für ein erfolgreiches Studium wissen und können muss* (3., vollst. überarb. u. akt. Aufl.). *UTB Schlüsselkompetenzen: Vol. 4748*. Verlag Ferdinand Schöningh.

Goldenstein, J., Hunoldt, M., & Walgenbach, P. (2018). *Wissenschaftliche(s) Arbeiten in den Wirtschaftswissenschaften*. Springer Fachmedien. https://doi.org/10.1007/978-3-658-20345-0.

Guba, B. (2008). Systematische Literatursuche [Systematic literature search]. *Wiener medizinische Wochenschrift, 158*(1–2), 62–69. https://doi.org/10.1007/s10354-007-0500-0.

Kindler, H., Weber, F., Kühne, O., & Halder, G. (2019). *Wissenschaftlich arbeiten in Geographie und Raumwissenschaften: Ein Überblick*. Springer Essentials.

Kornmeier, M. (2024). *Wissenschaftlich schreiben leicht gemacht: Für Bachelor, Master und Dissertation* (10th ed.). *UTB Schlüsselkompetenzen: Vol. 3154*. utb. https://doi.org/10.36198/9783838562070.

Oehlrich, M. (2014). *Wissenschaftliches Arbeiten und Schreiben: Schritt für Schritt zur Bachelor- und Master-Thesis in den Wirtschaftswissenschaften*. Springer. https://doi.org/10.1007/978-3-662-44099-5.

Prexl, L. (2019). *Mit digitalen Quellen arbeiten: Richtig zitieren aus Datenbanken, E-Books, YouTube & Co* (3., aktualisierte und überarbeitete Aufl.). *UTB Schlüsselkompetenzen: Vol. 4420*. Verlag Ferdinand Schöningh. https://doi.org/10.36198/9783838550725.

Schryen, G. (2015). Writing qualitative IS literature reviews—guidelines for synthesis, interpretation, and guidance of research. *Communications of the Association for Information Systems, 37*. https://doi.org/10.17705/1CAIS.03712.

Snyder, H. (2019). Literature review as a research methodology: An overview and guidelines. *Journal of Business Research, 104*, 333–339. https://doi.org/10.1016/j.jbusres.2019.07.039.

7 Writing: AI in Text Creation

Abstract

This chapter analyzes the use of artificial intelligence (AI) in the academic writing process. Support ranges from structuring the work and developing individual chapters to formulating and optimizing language. AI systems are particularly helpful in developing argumentation structures, overcoming writer's block, and improving linguistic style. The chapter presents various prompts and application scenarios that enable users to create outlines, elaborate microstructures, or critically reflect on existing texts. The role of AI as a tool to foster independent thinking and argumentative precision is emphasized. The examples demonstrate how AI can serve effectively as a writing coach and analytical assistant without replacing the creative and reflective contributions of the writer. The aim is to make academic writing more productive, structured, and of higher quality by combining human expertise with machine support.

"Writing is thinking. To write well is to think clearly. That's why it's so hard."
– David McCullough (2002, p. 53)

7.1 Integration of AI into the Academic Writing Process

Current studies show that AI-generated texts are, in many respects, structurally more coherent and linguistically more sophisticated than many texts written by humans. In a study comparing 90 essays by German upper secondary students with texts produced by ChatGPT-3 and ChatGPT-4, the AI texts received significantly better ratings—especially in the categories of logic and structure, language proficiency, complexity, vocabulary, and textual cohesion (Herbold et al., 2023). A similar study with education students yielded comparable results. Here, AI-generated texts performed better in criteria such as logic and language proficiency as well. In

F. Lang, *Using Artificial Intelligence in Term Papers and Theses*,
https://doi.org/10.1007/978-3-662-73208-3_7

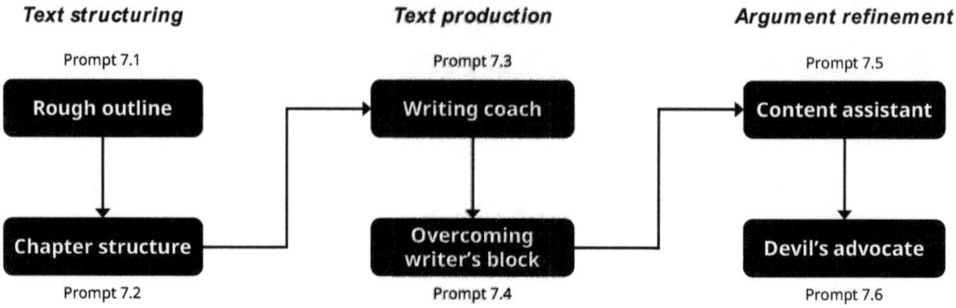

Fig. 7.1 Writing academic texts with AI

the areas of expressiveness, sentence complexity, vocabulary, and textual cohesion, however, there were no significant differences compared to the students' texts. The participants' own perceptions are also interesting: they rated the use of AI as helpful, primarily for idea generation, structuring the text, and building a coherent argument. AI was also experienced as useful for overcoming writer's block. It was considered less effective, however, for avoiding errors and for precisely formulating individual statements (Tengler & Brandhofer, 2025).

In academic practice, AI is therefore increasingly seen as a supplement to human writing—not as a replacement, but as a supportive tool for improving style, structure, and argumentative logic. Figure 7.1 illustrates how AI can support the writing process at these points—from the initial outline to critical reflection.

7.2 Structuring

A coherent argument is a key success factor in academic work. It ensures that ideas are developed in a comprehensible way and presented convincingly. To achieve this, content must be clearly organized and structured in a way that is consistently maintained throughout the entire paper. This external structure is usually reflected in the outline. It provides a framework within which the argument can unfold and helps readers to follow the thread of the work. Within this framework, the so-called internal structure emerges—the actual text, in which ideas are elaborated in detail and interconnected. Only through the interplay of external order and internal argumentation does a paper become both comprehensible and academically convincing (Kornmeier, 2024).

The outline should not be seen as a rigid construct. Rather, it evolves during the course of working on the topic—in parallel with the substantive engagement with the subject. New insights, changes in perspective, or refinements of the research question may require restructuring existing chapters or adding new sections. A good outline is therefore not only well thought out, but also flexible enough to appropriately reflect new findings (Oehlrich, 2014).

The outline of an academic paper serves a dual function: it is not only an expression of the argumentative structure, but also a concrete plan for the writing process. Even at an early stage of topic development, it provides initial orientation points regarding the focus of the content. This is precisely where many students face a challenge: how should the available pages be sensibly distributed among the individual chapters? This question cannot be answered in general terms, as the weighting of individual sections depends on several factors. In addition to discipline-specific conventions, the requirements of supervising instructors, the type of paper, and the respective degree program also play a role. For example, a term paper focuses more on a concise presentation of the topic, while a bachelor's thesis is expected to include more independent conclusions. In a master's thesis, methodological aspects often become more important, while formal requirements recede somewhat into the background (Winter, 2009).

Especially when developing an initial rough outline, the use of AI tools can be helpful. With a suitable prompt, not only can outline suggestions be generated, but initial estimates of the relative weighting of chapters can also be obtained. A dialog-based approach to creating a subject-specific outline was already explained in Sect. 5.6.

An alternative to this approach is shown in Prompt 7.1, which is designed to draft an initial chapter structure, gain a better understanding of the content, and develop a sense for the allocation of available pages. Here, the AI takes on the role of an experienced expert in academic writing and considers both thematic and methodological requirements. Based on the specified research question and planned page count, it creates a numbered outline, supplemented by brief explanations of the function and content of each chapter. In addition, it provides percentage recommendations for distributing the total length among the individual sections. The prompt thus promotes a better understanding of the structure, weighting, and argumentative logic of academic texts.

Prompt 7.1: Rough Outline and Initial Estimate of Chapter Length

Context

You are an experienced expert in academic writing and the structuring of scholarly texts. Your task is to support students in creating a well-founded and balanced chapter structure. The goal is to develop a structure that sensibly distributes the total length of an academic paper and takes into account the content relevance for the research question.

Instruction

Develop a chapter structure for an academic paper with a total length of approximately [number of pages] pages. The chapters should be designed to organize the content thematically and methodologically, clearly structure the research question, and facilitate reader guidance.

The underlying research question is: [research question]

Specifications

- Present the chapters in numbered order (e.g., 1. Introduction, 2. Theoretical Background, etc.).
- Indicate the recommended number of pages for each chapter as a percentage of the total length (e.g., 10% of 50 pages = 5 pages).
- Add a brief description to each chapter explaining its function, the type of content, and key aspects to consider.
- Use a clear format such as bullet points or numbered lists for better readability.

The result of such a prompt should always be understood as a first draft. The automatically generated structure requires critical review and further development based on one's own considerations, initial literature analyses, and content priorities. The suggested allocation of page numbers to chapters should also never be adopted uncritically. Instead, it should be checked whether this distribution meets the requirements of one's own work. Consulting with the supervisor is often useful in this context, in order to incorporate their experience and expectations into the development. In this way, an AI-supported draft becomes a well-considered, academically sound structure that forms the basis for a convincing academic report.

Once the rough outline has established the basic structure of the paper and thus prepared a clear thread, the focus shifts to the microstructure within the individual chapters. In this next step, the aim is to plan the detailed content of the chapters: How should a topic be introduced? Where should hypotheses be placed? What components belong in a chapter, and where should content priorities be set (Gansel et al., 2018)? These questions are crucial for the coherence and persuasiveness of the entire paper. It is important to consider which theoretical foundations, empirical findings, or methodological considerations—depending on the chapter—should be presented in which order to enable readers to follow a logical and well-structured line of thought. Working with notes and excerpts can be a great help in building the microstructure. They make it possible to organize ideas, filter out central arguments, and identify initial connections. Especially in the early phase of writing, they facilitate getting started and help determine the content direction within a chapter (Wymann & Neff, 2018).

An example prompt for using AI to develop an initial draft for the microstructure of a chapter is shown in Prompt 7.2. Based on the respective research question as well as existing notes and excerpts, the AI suggests a possible structure for the chapter. This structure includes suggestions as to which thematic sections should be included in the chapter, the purpose of each section, and how much space each should take up. This approach is particularly helpful for thematically organizing already collected information, putting it in a logical order, and thus developing a clear thread within the chapter. The draft can thus facilitate the start of writing and create structural clarity.

As with the rough outline as macrostructure, it is also necessary to critically examine the AI-generated suggestion for the microstructure. Key questions include: Does the proposed structure meet the academic standards of the field? Does it cover all content-relevant aspects? And is the order of the sections logically consistent? Only if these points are carefully checked and, if necessary, adjusted through further AI support or one's own revision, will a coherent, academically appropriate line of argument emerge. In this way, AI does not become a substitute solution, but a productive source of inspiration in the writing process.

Prompt 7.2: Structural Idea for a Chapter

Context

You are an academic advisor with proven expertise in scholarly writing and chapter structuring. The goal is to develop a tried-and-tested structural template for the chapter [chapter name]. The structure should be based on academic publications, ensure a logical sequence, and clearly integrate the research question [research question]. The chapter should fit meaningfully into the overall structure of the paper: [complete outline].

Instruction

Develop a detailed structural template for the chapter [chapter name] that covers the central sections of this chapter. The content should build logically on one another and follow a coherent line of argument.

Take into account the following notes and/or excerpts:
[notes or excerpts]

Specifications

- Divide the chapter into clearly defined sections with specific functions.
- Provide a brief description of the function and content of each section.
- Estimate the length of each section as a percentage of the total chapter length.
- Use a clear and concise format, such as bullet points or numbered lists.

7.3 Text Production

When it comes to actually writing the research report, it is usually helpful to consciously set aside perfectionism at first. At the beginning, the focus should be less on linguistic subtleties or content details and more on the flow of writing. The goal of this writing phase is to capture thoughts as unfiltered as possible—including those that arise spontaneously or are inspired by previous reading. The productive collection and formulation of ideas is thus the priority, not the immediate creation of a print-ready text. In a second step, targeted revision is carried out to sharpen the argument, identify logical breaks, and clarify contradictions. Transitions are smoothed, central statements are strengthened, and content relevance is critically reviewed. Consistency—that is, logic and coherence within and between sections—is also systematically ensured at this stage. In this way, an academic text is gradually created that is not only academically sound, but also convincing and easy to read (Wymann & Neff, 2018).

Once the content of the text is well coordinated and logically structured, the next step is to focus on linguistic expression. Now it is a matter of formulating the arguments in a manner appropriate to academic standards. The style is often shaped by the conventions and jargon of the respective discipline. Academic writing follows overarching quality criteria that are not only formal in nature, but serve the purpose of conveying content clearly and convincingly.

A good academic style is characterized by the fact that readers are not burdened with unnecessary words, truisms, or platitudes. Awkward and artificially inflated formulations are avoided, as is language that is either overloaded with jargon or flattened by excessive simplicity. In addition, stylistic inconsistencies should be avoided, as well as trendy terms or colloquial expressions (Esselborn-Krumbiegel, 2022; Franck, 2017). The aim is a precise, clear, and at the same time nuanced expression that does justice both to the subject and to the readership. Such a style is not an end in itself, but a necessary prerequisite for academic ideas to be communicated in a comprehensible, convincing, and effective manner.

AI can be used in a targeted way to optimize linguistic quality, as exemplified by the writing coach in Prompt 7.3. The goal is not only to improve the specific text, but also to develop one's own academic writing style in the long term.

Prompt 7.3: Writing Coach

Context

You are a writing coach with proven expertise in linguistic precision, technical style, and academic writing. The goal is to optimize texts so that they are precise, comprehensible, and stylistically adapted to the respective field. At the same time, unnecessarily complex formulations should be simplified without losing content depth or academic accuracy. The optimization should also help me to improve my own academic writing skills in the long term.

Instruction

Optimize the given text by suggesting more precise formulations and adapting the style to the requirements of a professional audience. Identify overly complex sentences and reduce their complexity without compromising academic rigor or expressiveness. Add, where necessary, notes on stylistic adjustments relevant to the respective field.

Specifications

1. More precise formulations
   - List alternative formulations that are more precise and clearer.
   - Present the original formulation and the revised version side by side.
2. Field-specific style advice
   - Provide tips on how to adapt the style to the respective field (e.g., tone, technical terms, avoidance of colloquial language).
   - Justify stylistic adjustments with reference to typical conventions of the respective discipline.
3. Reducing complexity
   - Identify overly complex or convoluted sentences.
   - Suggest simplified versions that remain equivalent in content.
   - Explain, if necessary, why the simplification is useful (e.g., better readability, clearer argumentation).

The output should be presented in a clearly structured and organized form, e.g., using numbered lists or sections with headings.

All changes or suggestions should be transparent and justified. The aim is for me to recognize where and why improvements are needed, so that I can learn from them.

AI supports this process by suggesting more precise formulations, reducing excessive complexity, and adapting the style to the linguistic conventions of the respective field. In doing so, it ensures that content depth and academic accuracy are maintained, while readability and argumentative clarity are improved. For all changes, the AI provides transparent and didactically prepared justifications. In this way, students not only receive concrete assistance for their current text, but also develop a better understanding of linguistic impact, appropriate academic expression, and stylistic nuances.

To remain productive in academic writing, it is crucial to achieve a continuous writing flow. This flow experience is closely linked to three central conditions that make writing not only more efficient, but also a rewarding experience (Esselborn-Krumbiegel, 2015; Swoboda, 2023):

First, writing flow requires an appropriate match between the demands of the writing task and one's own abilities. If the demands are too high, this can lead to overwhelm, causing the writing process to stall. Conversely, if the demands are too low, boredom and a lack of mental stimulation threaten, which impairs concentration and content depth. In both cases, writer's block can occur—that is, the feeling of being unable to continue writing or not finding a suitable starting point. Second, setting clear goals is crucial. Those who know exactly what is required, which rules must be followed, and what is important academically can work more purposefully. Feedback—such as from instructors or by analyzing successful sample papers—helps to sharpen one's own goals and calibrate the text. Third, the perceived control over the writing process plays a central role. Those who feel they have the process under control write with more confidence and inner calm. In the face of impending overwhelm, simple strategies can help: such as creating structural sketches, reducing the material used, or breaking down complex tasks into smaller, manageable steps.

If writer's block occurs, the use of AI can help to reflect on the causes in a targeted way and to develop suitable strategies for overcoming it, in order to restore writing flow. With targeted prompts, for example, mental blocks can be analyzed, structuring suggestions developed, or alternative ways to start the text can be found. Prompt 7.4 exemplifies how AI can function as a dialogical writing coach in such situations.

Prompt 7.4: Overcoming Writer's Block

Context

You are an expert in academic writing with a focus on writing processes, mental blocks, and individual strategies for text development. The goal is to work together with the affected person to identify the type of block and develop a tailored solution—step by step and oriented to the specific writing situation.

Instruction

Accompany the writer in analyzing their writer's block and developing individual solution strategies. Start with a brief problem clarification: ask up to five precise reflection questions to find out in which phase of writing the block occurs (e.g., at the beginning, during structuring or formulating), how it manifests itself, what thoughts or emotions are associated with it, what has already been tried, and what has been helpful in the past. The aim is to identify typical thought patterns or external conditions that hinder writing flow.

Based on this, develop a tailored strategy for overcoming the block. The recommendations should be concrete, practical, and adapted to the stated situation. Choose suitable methods such as freewriting for entry barriers, mind maps for structuring, deliberately imperfect writing for perfectionism, or scheduled writing sessions for procrastination. Add, if necessary, supportive elements such as rituals, mental writing contracts, or simple exercises to activate the writing process.

Specifications

- Use clear language, short paragraphs, lists, and subheadings.
- Address directly (using "you"), in a motivating and solution-oriented manner.
- Do not offer general theory, but individual support on an equal footing.

Table 7.1 Further Approaches for Writing Assistance with AI

Writing Assistance	Description
Developing balanced sentence lengths	The AI analyzes text passages for unbalanced sentence structures and suggests shortening or expanding them to improve reading flow and avoid monotony
Creating smooth transitions	The AI provides suitable formulations for transitions between sections or argumentative steps to strengthen coherence in the text and avoid leaps in logic
Expanding precise vocabulary	The AI suggests context-appropriate alternatives to frequently used words, helping to vary vocabulary without sacrificing accuracy
Finding stylistically appropriate formulations	The AI offers alternative ways of expressing existing sentences—for example, for awkward phrases, passive constructions, or linguistic vagueness
Targeted avoidance of repetition	The AI detects duplicate terms or formulations and suggests stylistically varied alternatives to avoid redundancy
Ensuring stylistic consistency	The AI checks whether the writing style within a text remains consistent—for example, in terms of tone, technical language, or sentence structure—and provides targeted feedback on breaks or inconsistencies

In doing so, the AI draws on proven principles of writing consultation: through targeted reflection questions, it helps to classify the individual block—such as by its phase of origin, typical thought patterns, or accompanying emotions. On this basis, it develops a tailored strategy for overcoming the block, which can draw on concrete methods such as freewriting, mind mapping, or pressure-reducing writing. The dialogical character of the prompt not only supports problem solving, but also encourages independent reflection on one's own writing process.

The possibilities for AI support in writing are extremely diverse. Even at the level of individual sentences or terms, targeted prompts can yield improvements that positively impact the comprehensibility, style, and persuasiveness of a text. These fine adjustments—from word choice to transitions to sentence structure—often make a big difference in the end result. Table 7.1 provides an overview of further possible uses of AI in the writing process. The ideas listed there range from stylistic fine-tuning to the structural optimization of entire sections and show how differentiated and at the same time practical AI tools can be used to specifically improve academic texts.

7.4 Argumentation

Writing is much more than simply recording already finished thoughts—it is an active process of thinking. Only through writing do thoughts take shape, connections become apparent, and one's own positions become clearer. The development of a coherent argumentation therefore does not occur solely in advance, but often only during the act of writing itself.

In contrast to spoken language, which is closely tied to the moment and the speaker, written sentences stand on their own. They can be read, understood, and critically questioned independently of the author. This independence allows for a higher degree of abstraction and theoretical thinking. In addition, writing relieves the burden on short-term memory: ideas do not have to be remembered, evaluated, and formulated all at once, but can be processed, reconsidered, and further developed one after the other. This makes it possible to reorder arguments, compare different ideas, or deliberately improve formulations (Menary, 2007).

Those who write, think—and those who write consciously sharpen their arguments in the process. This is precisely why content reflection is so valuable for writing. Thus, writing is not only a means of presentation, but also a tool for clarifying and further developing one's own thoughts.

In this respect, the use of AI in this context should primarily serve to further develop one's own analytical skills and to critically question the text. Especially in terms of content engagement, an intelligent writing assistant can help to check arguments, identify gaps in reasoning, or open up new perspectives. Prompt 7.5 provides an example of how AI can be used in this role—not as an automated substitute for one's own thinking, but as a source of inspiration for reflective and well-founded argumentative writing.

Prompt 7.5: Writing Assistant for Content Engagement

Context

You are a writing assistant with proven expertise in the critical analysis and synthesis of academic texts. The goal is to systematically penetrate the text, identify key statements, and critically review your own interpretation through targeted self-reflection.

Instruction

Assist in analyzing a given text by:

1. Developing self-reflection questions that encourage critical engagement with the text (e.g., argumentative strength, missing aspects) and question your own stance and interpretation (e.g., "To what extent do my prior experiences influence my understanding of the text?").
2. Extracting the key statements of the text and summarizing them concisely. For each, explain why these statements are central to understanding the text.
3. Formulating a text synthesis that bundles the essential content. Compare this with the key statements to ensure that all important points have been considered.

Specifications

- Present the analysis in a clearly structured and organized manner, e.g., using numbered lists or sections with subheadings.

- The content should be precisely formulated and easy to follow, so that it can be directly used for self-reflection and text evaluation.
- The work steps should be designed not only to analyze the specific text, but also to help strengthen one's own analytical skills.

In this prompt, the AI acts as an analytical writing assistant, helping to identify, precisely formulate, and critically reflect on the key statements of one's own text. Through targeted self-reflection questions, writers are encouraged to systematically question the structure of their argumentation, possible gaps, and their own interpretation. A concluding synthesis concisely summarizes the essential statements and thus provides a clear overview of the text. On this basis, it is possible to check whether one's own thoughts are fully, with appropriate balance, and with the desired emphasis represented in the text.

An effective strategy for checking the consistency and persuasiveness of one's own thoughts is the so-called principle of the Advocatus Diaboli (Devil's Advocate)—thinking in counterpositions. In this thought experiment, one deliberately takes on the role of a critical counterpart and actively seeks objections, weaknesses, and alternative viewpoints. Through this controversial engagement, one gains new perspectives on one's own argumentation, can further develop it in a targeted manner, and respond to possible counterarguments at an early stage. In this way, not only is the argumentative depth of one's own text strengthened, but also its resilience in academic discourse. In Prompt 7.6, the AI simulates the role of an Advocatus Diaboli: The AI develops potential objections, anticipates critical perspectives from different groups, and helps to formulate convincing counterstrategies. This not only improves argumentative depth, but also fosters the ability to engage critically and reflectively with one's own text.

Prompt 7.6: Advocatus Diaboli

Context

You take on the role of an Advocatus Diaboli in order to deliberately challenge an existing argumentation. The goal is for you to identify potential weaknesses, anticipate critical perspectives, and develop well-thought-out counterstrategies. In this way, the argumentative substance can be deepened and prepared for possible objections.

Instruction

Support the analysis of an existing argumentation by:

1. Generating possible objections.

    - List counterarguments that could be raised on different levels (logical, ethical, emotional, practical) against the position taken.

- Add brief examples or scenarios that plausibly illustrate these objections.

2. Anticipating critical perspectives.

- Describe which groups of people or social actors might typically represent these objections (e.g., subject matter experts, political groups, affected target groups).
- Provide indications of how these perspectives could influence or dominate the discourse.

3. Developing strategies to strengthen your own position.

- Formulate clear and convincing responses to the objections raised.
- Provide recommendations on how the argumentation can be strengthened through additional facts, examples, comparisons, or rhetorical techniques.

Specifications

- The output should be presented in a structured and clear manner, e.g., through numbered lists or sections with subheadings.
- The content should be precisely formulated and easy to follow.
- Arguments, examples, and counterstrategies should be logically structured and easy to follow.
- Optional: Emphases (e.g., bolding) can be used to clearly highlight key points or contrasts.

7.5 Do's and Don'ts

Do's

1. *Maintain personal responsibility*: Treat every AI output as raw material and take responsibility for content, form, and sources.
2. *Critically review*: Check the logic, technical terms, citations, and facts of every AI-generated passage before including it in your work.
3. *Use structure as a starting point*: Use AI-generated outlines as a starting point; adjust structure, emphasis, and order based on your own findings.
4. *Revise iteratively*: Alternate between draft text, AI optimization, and your own revision until coherence and consistency are achieved.
5. *Sharpen linguistic precision*: Ask the AI for alternatives, shortenings, or simplifications to keep technical language clear, concise, and consistent.
6. *Test arguments*: Have a "Devil's Advocate" formulate objections to strengthen the depth of reasoning and discussion skills.
7. *Resolve blockages*: Use AI as a dialogical writing coach to maintain flow and motivation.

Don'ts

1. *Uncritical adoption:* Do not include AI-generated sections verbatim without your own review; do not trust supposed studies, citations, or figures provided by the AI.
2. *Outsourcing thinking:* Do not use AI as a substitute for your own analysis, interpretation, or argument development, but only as a supplement and source of inspiration.
3. *Expecting a one-pass result:* Do not assume that the first AI output is ready for submission; revision cycles, including manual ones, are essential.
4. *Skipping human feedback:* Do not forgo feedback from fellow students and supervisors—AI does not replace expert critique.

References

Esselborn-Krumbiegel, H. (2015). *Tipps und Tricks bei Schreibblockaden. Stark fürs Studium: Vol. 4318*. Verlag Ferdinand Schöningh. https://doi.org/10.36198/9783838555690.

Esselborn-Krumbiegel, H. (2022). *Richtig wissenschaftlich schreiben: Wissenschaftssprache in Regeln und Übungen* (7th ed.). *Uni Tipps: Vol. 3429*. Verlag Ferdinand Schöningh. https://doi.org/10.36198/9783838558639.

Franck, N. (2017). *Handbuch wissenschaftliches Arbeiten: Was man für ein erfolgreiches Studium wissen und können muss* (3rd ed.). *UTB Schlüsselkompetenzen: Vol. 4748*. Verlag Ferdinand Schöningh. https://doi.org/10.36198/9783838547480.

Gansel, C., Jesan, I., Kovtunova, E., Nefedov, S., Ros, G., & Schäfer, P. (2018). Textorganisation. In C. Gansel & S. T. Nefedov (Eds.), *Wissenschaftliches Schreiben: Ein Handbuch*. Ernst-Moritz-Arndt-Universität.

Herbold, S., Hautli-Janisz, A., Heuer, U., Kikteva, Z., & Trautsch, A. (2023). A large-scale comparison of human-written versus ChatGPT-generated essays. *Scientific Reports, 13*(1), 18617. https://doi.org/10.1038/s41598-023-45644-9.

Kornmeier, M. (2024). *Wissenschaftlich schreiben leicht gemacht: Für Bachelor, Master und Dissertation (10., aktual. u. erg. Aufl.). UTB Schlüsselkompetenzen: Vol. 3154*. utb. https://doi.org/10.36198/9783838562070.

McCullough, D. (2002). The danger of historical amnesia. *Humanities, 23*(4) (Interview with Bruce Cole).

Menary, R. (2007). Writing as thinking. *Language Sciences, 29*(5), 621–632. https://doi.org/10.1016/j.langsci.2007.01.005.

Oehlrich, M. (2014). *Wissenschaftliches Arbeiten und Schreiben: Schritt für Schritt zur Bachelor- und Master-Thesis in den Wirtschaftswissenschaften*. Springer. https://doi.org/10.1007/978-3-662-44099-5.

Swoboda, M. (2023). *Wissenschaftlich schreiben leicht gemacht: Ein Leitfaden für Architektur- und Designstudiengänge*. Springer Vieweg. https://doi.org/10.1007/978-3-658-42166-3.

Tengler, K., & Brandhofer, G. (2025). KI oder nicht KI? *Medienimpulse, 63*(1) https://doi.org/10.21243/MI-01-25-11.

Winter, W. (2009). *Wissenschaftliche Arbeiten schreiben: Hausarbeiten; Seminar- und Projektarbeiten; Bachelor- und Masterarbeiten; Dissertationen* (*New Business Line Arbeitstechniken*, 3. ed.). REDLINE-Verlag.

Wymann, C., & Neff, F. (2018). *Checkliste Schreibprozess: Ihr Weg zum guten Text: Punkt für Punkt. UTB Schlüsselkompetenzen: Vol. 4960*. Budrich. https://doi.org/10.36198/9783838549606.

Data: AI in Analysis

8

Abstract

This chapter examines how artificial intelligence (AI), in the form of large language models, can be used to support the process of empirical data analysis. The focus is on three key steps: selecting appropriate methods, evaluating and interpreting the data, and visualizing the results. The chapter demonstrates how AI can provide well-founded suggestions for method selection—both for qualitative and quantitative data—while also taking into account risks such as hallucinations or methodological deviations. In the second part, the chapter shows how AI can assist in the practical implementation and reflection of analytical procedures, without replacing the necessary scientific responsibility. Finally, it outlines ways in which AI can be applied to the creation of scientific visualizations—for example, through code generation for graphical tools. The aim of the chapter is to strengthen students' methodological competence and to enhance the quality of empirical work through targeted use of AI. Numerous prompts provide practical examples of how this approach can be implemented in concrete terms.

"Without data, you're just another person with an opinion."
– W. Edwards Deming (quoted in Kolasa et al., 2020, p. 147)

8.1 AI-Supported Data Analysis

While textbooks and online tutorials provide valuable foundational knowledge, the transition from theory to selecting the appropriate method for one's own dataset remains a challenge for many students. For this reason, the use of AI for data analysis is becoming increasingly popular—both for qualitative data, which are analyzed in a text-based and subjective-interpretive manner (e.g., interviews,

F. Lang, *Using Artificial Intelligence in Term Papers and Theses*,
https://doi.org/10.1007/978-3-662-73208-3_8

comments), and for quantitative data, which are numerical, measurable, and structured (e.g., surveys, key figures) (Ray, 2023).

Whereas traditional statistical software demonstrates its strengths primarily in the analysis of quantitative data, large language models show the opposite pattern: these models were primarily trained to process, understand, and generate language. Accordingly, they are particularly well suited to support the analysis of qualitative data, for example by assisting in the formulation of category systems, writing memos, or reflecting on interpretations.

For quantitative questions, however, AI in its purely language-based application initially reaches its limits. Since a language model is designed to predict the most likely next expression, it can make systematic errors in mathematical calculations or counting tasks. A frequently cited example is the question of how many "r"s are in the English word "Strawberry." Even after repeated attempts, language models sometimes provide incorrect answers—sometimes with surprising persistence. One reason for this is that language models work with tokens, i.e., frequent letter sequences, instead of individual letters (Conde et al., 2025).

Despite these weaknesses in numerical tasks, AI models are by no means useless for quantitative questions—on the contrary. Their strength lies in their ability to write and execute code, for example in the widely used programming language Python, which plays a central role in data science. If a language-based answer is incorrect, a targeted prompt to solve the task using code can often lead to the correct solution. In this way, the weaknesses of the language model can be compensated for by its computational abilities in the form of code.

The behavior of AI collides with the requirements of science in several respects. For example, the fact that AI responses can vary greatly makes it difficult to reliably replicate scientific analyses. In addition, many AI models are so-called "black boxes," meaning the exact decision-making process remains opaque. This limits transparency in methodological decisions. Furthermore, hidden biases in the model or data can jeopardize the integrity of research results (Perkins & Roe, 2024). These factors contradict key principles of good scientific practice and make it clear that AI systems must not be used uncritically or without scrutiny in research contexts. Especially in empirical research, it is of fundamental importance that researchers can trace and understand exactly what was analyzed and how each analytical step was carried out.

Accordingly, the role of AI in data analysis should primarily be supportive in nature. Language models can help explain methodological concepts, identify common errors, or suggest alternative analytical paths. In doing so, they foster methodological understanding, but do not replace the necessary methodological self-responsibility—that is, the ability to make decisions in the research process consciously, reflectively, and based on professional standards. If AI tools are used merely as automatic problem solvers without applying one's own methodological judgment, this undermines the scientific quality of the work. However, if they are used as learning and reflection tools, they can help sharpen scientific judgment, expand analytical skills, and specifically improve the quality of empirical research (Karras et al., 2024).

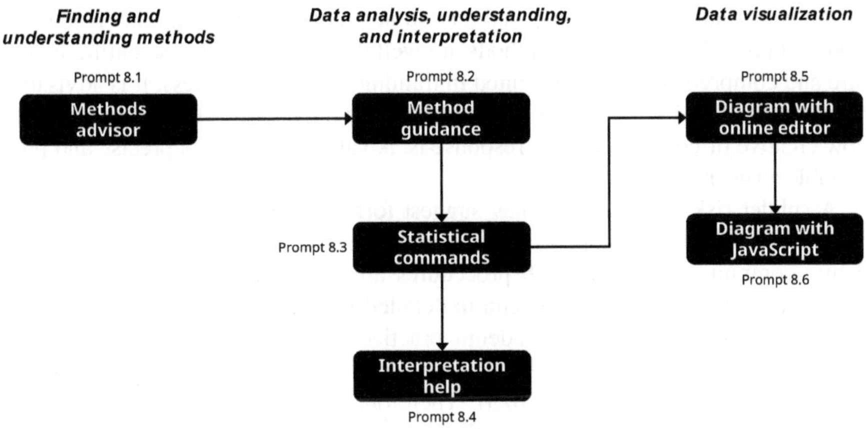

Fig. 8.1 Data analysis with AI

This chapter addresses the question of how AI can be meaningfully integrated into the empirical research process. The focus is on the following three sub-areas: 1. Selecting and understanding appropriate methods, 2. analyzing, interpreting, and reflecting on data, and 3. visualizing results. Figure 8.1 shows the relationship of the prompts in this chapter.

8.2 Finding and Understanding Methods

Empirical data only yield insights if they are analyzed using an appropriate methodological approach. When making this decision, students often rely on classic aids—such as statistics textbooks, methodological literature, or online tutorials. One helpful tool for statistical methods is the decision tree from the Methods Consulting Service at the University of Zurich (Schwarz, 2025), which guides users step by step to the appropriate analysis method. Nevertheless, selecting suitable procedures remains a challenge for many. Textbooks often convey rather theoretical and abstract content, which can seem difficult to apply in practice. The concrete implementation—that is, the bridge between theory and empirical application—often remains unclear.

Artificial intelligence can noticeably facilitate this decision-making process by providing well-founded suggestions for selecting and applying appropriate analytical procedures. This involves, on the one hand, content fit—that is, ensuring that the proposed procedure matches the research objective, the type of data, and the research question. On the other hand, it is crucial that the procedure is implemented correctly, meaning all necessary assumptions are considered and the steps are carried out without error. This support is possible for both quantitative and qualitative data. At the same time, potential risks must also be considered. As with all generative AI applications, there is a risk of hallucinations, for example when methods or statements are suggested that do not actually exist. This risk is low for standard procedures, as these methods are well documented in the scientific literature and comprehensively represented in training data. Nevertheless, it is advisable to adjust the LLM temperature in the chat. The temperature of an LLM controls how creative or conservative the response is. A value of 0 ensures precise and predictable answers.

A subtler risk is that the AI may suggest formally correct but uncommon procedures that do not correspond to the accepted standard within a particular academic community. Even if such procedures are not fundamentally wrong, their application can be confusing or require detailed justification to be understandable to reviewers or supervisors. In academic practice, it is often advisable to use established procedures, as these are better understood and accepted within the respective discipline (Watson et al., 2025). Therefore, AI-supported method selection should always be critically examined. Students should actively engage with the proposed procedures—not only to check their plausibility, but also to develop a deeper understanding of the methodological logic and the requirements for correct application. The same applies here: AI is a tool that supports scientific work, but does not replace critical thinking in the research process.

An exemplary prompt that helps in selecting suitable procedures is shown in Prompt 8.1. It demonstrates how a virtual method advisor can be configured to recommend appropriate methods based on the research objective, research question, and data structure.

Prompt 8.1: Method Advisor for Data Analysis

Context

You are an experienced professor whose goal is to competently, clearly, and practically advise students on their thesis projects. The focus is on selecting appropriate statistical methods that are both scientifically sound and understandable for students to apply.

Instruction

My research question is: Does exercise lower blood sugar, and if so, by how much?

Advise me on selecting a suitable method for the statistical analysis of a dataset. The dataset includes blood sugar measurements from 100 people—50 of whom performed a 30-minute exercise after the first measurement, while the other 50 rested during this time. Afterwards, all had their blood sugar measured again. The following variables are also available: gender, age, and body mass index (BMI).

1. Recommend suitable statistical methods to answer the research question and outline the basic idea of each method.
2. Discuss the advantages and disadvantages of the proposed methods.

3. State the prerequisites for their correct application and show how I can best check these prerequisites.
4. Finally, provide a concrete recommendation as to which method is best suited for this study design under which circumstances.

Specifications

- Present the advantages and disadvantages of the proposed methods in a table.
- Create a ranking of the methods for the recommendation, including justification for each placement.
- The language should be clear, didactic, and student-friendly—the goal is for students to not only apply the recommendations but also understand them.
- The suggestions should be based on common statistical practice in empirical theses.

The prompt first describes the goal of the analysis, the academic background, and the underlying data. As an alternative to a textual description, a structured presentation of the data can also be attached to the prompt. In some cases, it is also useful to provide the actual raw data as an attachment to give the AI a solid analytical basis.

The goal of AI support should not be to prescribe a single method, but to present various suitable procedures with their respective advantages and disadvantages. This promotes independent decision-making by students and strengthens scientific reflection skills. Responsibility for methodological selection thus remains with the human, ensuring that the research process is actively and consciously shaped.

A key element of such prompts is specifying the prerequisites for applying certain methods. This enables users to independently check whether the available data meet the methodological requirements. Especially for statistical procedures, formal assumptions—such as scale level, normal distribution, or homogeneity of variance—are crucial for the validity of the results. Accordingly, the AI should also explain procedures for checking these prerequisites, such as suitable tests or diagnostic graphics. For qualitative research methods, formal quality criteria also play a role in ensuring transparency and traceability of the analysis steps. For example, interrater reliability can be used to assess agreement between different codings, while documentation of the coding process, theoretical grounding of categories, and reflection on the researcher's own role are further central quality criteria (Olmos-Vega et al., 2022).

A particular advantage arises from the dialog-oriented format of AI assistants: if there are comprehension problems, targeted follow-up questions can be asked and unclear aspects explained in more detail. Although there is always a risk of hallucinations, experience so far shows that the quality of methodological suggestions often exceeds the level of typical methodological knowledge among students, especially those who struggle with the subject. Nevertheless, it is essential to always critically review the AI's output and validate it using scientific sources. This has the added benefit that, in the course of this review, directly citable literature can be identified and used in one's own work.

8.3 Analyzing, Understanding, and Interpreting Data

Once a suitable method has been selected, the next step is to apply it correctly and interpret the results appropriately. AI can play a supportive role in this process by not only helping to select the method but also providing a step-by-step guide to practical implementation. It can explain typical procedures, point out possible pitfalls, and, if necessary, provide background knowledge on individual methodological steps.

Prompt 8.2 illustrates this approach using the example of a qualitative research method and shows how AI can be used to guide students through the methodological process—from preparation to execution to interpretation of results.

Prompt 8.2: Method Guide

Context

You are an experienced researcher who has conducted numerous studies using qualitative content analysis. The goal is to support students in the correct application of this method.

Instruction

I plan to analyze my transcribed interviews using Mayring's qualitative content analysis. Please provide me with the following:

1. A list of quality criteria that I must generally observe
2. A list of scientific literature that explains the methodology
3. A step-by-step guide distilled from the literature, with references
4. Notes on risks and pitfalls in applying the method
5. At least three sample prompts for how I can use AI to ensure the quality of my analysis process

Specifications

- Use only scientific sources that are citable in academic work.
- The step-by-step guide should be clearly structured and comprehensible, ideally with concrete examples.
- The notes on risks and pitfalls should be practical and highlight common sources of error.
- The AI prompts should be formulated so that they can be used directly in common AI chatbots.

Before the AI provides a concrete step-by-step guide for applying a method, the prompt should explicitly refer to the fundamental quality criteria of scientific research. These not only ensure methodological integrity but also promote method-conscious work and critical reflection on one's own approach.

Especially with qualitative methods, it is particularly important that students engage intensively with the relevant academic literature. These procedures are strongly shaped by individual interpretations, theoretical perspectives, and the active role of the researcher in the analysis. Therefore, given the capabilities of current models, it is not sufficient to rely solely on an automated guide from an AI system. Artificial intelligence can be used supportively—for example, through structured presentations of methodological procedures or notes on common sources of error—but it by no means replaces independent understanding of methodological fundamentals and critical reflection on key quality criteria.

In the field of quantitative research, especially in statistics, the requirements are more standardized and the risks of misapplication by AI are generally lower. Nevertheless, it is also advisable here to critically question the AI's output and compare it with suitable academic literature. This mainly concerns the choice of statistical tests, the interpretation of results, and understanding the underlying assumptions.

Only when there is a basic understanding of these framework conditions should the prompt move on to the actual implementation of the method. At this point, it is especially important not to regard the AI's result as the final solution. Instead, students should take the opportunity to ask targeted follow-up questions, allowing themselves to be actively guided through the analysis process and gradually build a deeper understanding of the methods. Only in this way can it be ensured that the methodological implementation is not blindly adopted, but is consciously understood and the student's own responsibility is maintained.

Another critical point is that AI models occasionally incorporate content from unverifiable or unreliable sources and falsely present them as scientifically sound. Hallucinated academic sources are regularly cited that do not actually exist. Therefore, it is essential to back up results with trustworthy literature.

Finally, the prompt asks for two additional elements: First, it should specifically mention risks and common pitfalls of the chosen method to help identify and consciously avoid methodological errors early on. Second, sample prompts should be formulated that can be used to check one's own analysis process.

For quantitative methods, AI demonstrates its potential particularly well, as statistical procedures are based on clearly defined, formalized structures. In the field of statistical software, there are basically two types: on the one hand, programs with a graphical user interface, such as SPSS or the open-source alternative Jamovi, which are mainly operated with the mouse. On the other hand, there are script-based statistical or programming languages such as R or Python, in which analyses are performed by entering code in a console.

It is precisely in these script-based environments that AI shows its strengths: it can generate statistical analyses in the form of executable code with precision, providing significant relief—for example, through automated calculations, model comparisons, or visualizations. Many programs with a graphical interface also have integrated script modes, such as SPSS syntax or the Rj editor in Jamovi, which allow text commands to be executed directly.

An example of how a prompt can be designed to generate a complete code snippet that performs a series of statistical tests is shown in Prompt 8.3.

Prompt 8.3: Creating Statistical Commands

Context

You are an experienced data scientist and are supporting me in the statistical analysis of my empirical thesis. I surveyed 200 people about their intention to use an AI assistant. In addition, their perceptions of usefulness and ease of use were recorded. These variables are now to be analyzed using multiple linear regression.

Instruction

```
Please write a complete R script that works with the following
data structure:> str(daten)
'data.frame': 324 obs. of 3 variables:
$ NI: num 0.25 -1.07 0.585 0.25 0.25 …
$ WN: num 0.181 -0.883 0.181 -0.522 0.181 …
$ WB: num -0.525 -1.834 -0.525 -0.525 -1.4 …
```

The script should implement four points:

1. Descriptive analysis of the variables: mean, median, standard deviation, variance, interquartile range, quartiles
2. Graphical representation of the distributions: histograms for each variable and a combined boxplot
3. Testing the assumptions of multiple linear regression (Gauss-Markov assumptions) including tests: linearity (scatterplots), independence of errors (Durbin-Watson test), homoscedasticity (Breusch-Pagan test), normality of residuals (Shapiro-Wilk test), multicollinearity (VIF)
   Please write a brief comment for each, indicating from which threshold or p-value the assumptions are considered met.
4. Calculation of the multiple linear regression with output of the model and results

Specifications

- The output should be presented as a commented R code snippet in a code box.

- Comments should be formulated so that even students without in-depth statistical knowledge can understand the code.
- The script output should be clear and modular (one section per objective).
- Only base functions and well-known R packages should be used.

The result of this prompt is a complete R script that automates most of the analysis. With the data structure provided to the AI, such a script is usually executable without prior adjustment—either step by step or as a whole. For programs with a graphical user interface such as SPSS or Jamovi, the AI can alternatively provide a step-by-step guide that describes exactly which menus to open and which options to select to manually achieve the desired result. This is especially helpful for beginners to understand the software's logic.

Many AI chatbots are also able to generate or execute Python code directly. Since Python is a widely used language in data analysis, almost all statistical procedures relevant to students are available there. In some cases, the AI can even perform calculations and output results directly. As tempting as this convenience may seem, such an approach is problematic from a scientific perspective. If the calculations are completely taken over by the AI and only the results are presented, traceability suffers. The human becomes increasingly passive in this process, resulting in a loss of methodological responsibility and critical questioning. Faulty results could be adopted uncritically, without understanding or checking how they were produced. This is precisely what must be avoided in scientific work. Therefore, it is essential to actively follow the calculation steps oneself—regardless of whether they are performed using R, Python, or a graphical interface. The AI can provide support, but it must not completely replace one's own analysis process.

After carrying out a method—whether qualitative or quantitative—the next challenge for students is to interpret the results correctly. Especially in statistics, uncertainty is common: the meanings of individual metrics are not always known or are misunderstood, which can lead to incorrect conclusions.

At this point, AI can be helpful in two ways. First, it can act as a kind of methodological fact-checker: students can enter their own interpretations of results in their own words and have the AI critically check whether they are logically correct. This sharpens understanding and reduces the risk of misinterpretation. Second, it is possible to provide the AI with a screenshot of the statistical software, such as a results table from SPSS, Jamovi, or R. Based on this, the AI can explain what is shown, which metrics are important, and how they can be interpreted in the given context. This helps to specifically reduce uncertainty. An example of such an explanation of a screenshot is shown in Prompt 8.4.

Prompt 8.4: Interpretation Aid

Context

You are a statistics lecturer with many years of experience supervising empirical theses. The goal is to enable me, as a student, to provide a clear but academically sound interpretation of my regression analysis so that I can correctly classify and explain the results in my thesis.

Instruction

I conducted a multiple linear regression to analyze the influence of perceived usefulness and ease of use on the intention to use an AI assistant. I have attached the regression output as a screenshot.

Please explain to me clearly and precisely:

1. The exact meaning of the p-values in the model: what do they say about the significance of the variables?
2. What the coefficient of determination R^2 and the adjusted R^2 indicate?
3. What the F-statistic measures and how it is interpreted?

Specifications

- Use clear, student-friendly language that is scientifically accurate but not unnecessarily complicated.
- Use illustrative examples or analogies to make more complex concepts (e.g., R^2 or p-value) more tangible.
- Where appropriate, provide interpretation aids or typical threshold values (e.g., $p < 0.05$ as a significance threshold), with source citation.
- Avoid pure definitions; the focus is on application and interpretation in the empirical study.

The prompt shown can be flexibly expanded and adapted to one's prior knowledge. Those who first want a comprehensive overview can, for example, ask the AI to explain the screenshot in full. Such basic requests are especially useful when building a fundamental understanding of the key metrics.

Even more effective, however, is the formulation of targeted questions, as included in the example prompt. These directly address existing uncertainties or knowledge gaps and enable a focused engagement with specific aspects of the analysis. This allows one's understanding to be deepened step by step and in a structured way, without being distracted by a multitude of irrelevant information.

Once the relevant points have been clarified, it is advisable to write an interpretation in one's own words. Afterwards, the AI can be used as a kind of fact-check: by submitting one's own interpretation and asking for feedback, content errors, imprecise terms, or logical misunderstandings can be identified and corrected early on.

In addition, the AI can also make further suggestions—for example, for quality assurance (e.g., robustness analyses) or for presenting the results (e.g., visualizations or tables). In this way, an AI-supported analysis process develops that expands one's own statistical skills and strengthens the methodological foundation of one's work.

8.4 Visualizing Data

In academic research, the clear presentation of relationships is a central element of knowledge transfer. Visualizations help structure complex content and increase the comprehensibility of scientific arguments. Traditionally, students and researchers rely on office products such as PowerPoint or Excel for this purpose. With the advent of artificial intelligence, new possibilities such as image generators have emerged. However, the current state of development of these technologies is not yet sufficient to visualize complex scientific results in an adequate form. Their use is currently limited to simple graphic representations, such as infographics, while the professional preparation of scientific visualizations still requires specialized tools and solid expertise.

Of greater practical relevance is the ability of current AI models to generate source code for visualizations. This code can be processed in specialized online editors that are based on a text-based description of graphic elements. Prominent examples include platforms such as RawGraphs.io, Draw.io, and Mermaid.live, which make it possible to create diagrams and charts based on structured data or source code. An example code with the resulting chart is shown in Fig. 8.2.

Artificial intelligence can provide valuable support here by directly generating markup code. This makes it possible to create precise visualizations based on textual descriptions and data. A practical application example can be found in Prompt 8.5, which demonstrates the design of a process diagram in Business Process

```
quadrantChart
   title Breast cancer diagnostic methods
   x-axis Low specificity --> High specificity
   y-axis Low sensitivity --> High sensitivity

   quadrant-1 Recommended
   quadrant-2 Many false alarms
   quadrant-3 Less useful
   quadrant-4 High non-detection

   "MRI": [0.61, 0.93]
   "3D": [0.75, 0.9999]
   "PET": [0.745, 0.885]
   "CT": [0.83, 0.71]
   "Ultrasound": [0.87, 0.61]
   "Mammography": [0.47, 0.72]
   "Thermography": [0.82, 0.39]
```

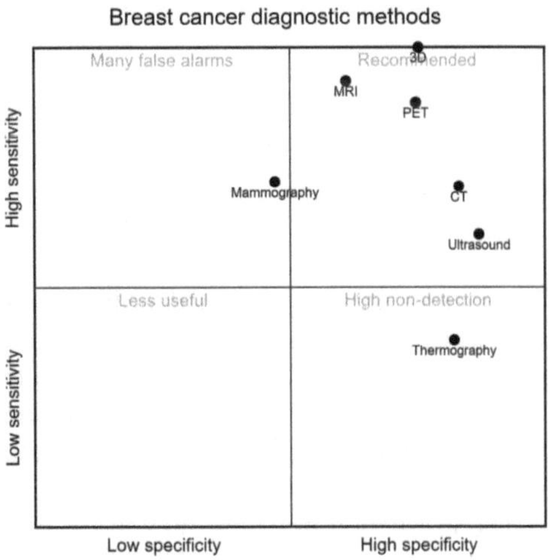

Fig. 8.2 Mermaid code and resulting figure. (Data from Lim et al., 2019)

Model and Notation (BPMN; Object Management Group, 2010) for use in the online editor Draw.io.

Prompt 8.5: Creating Diagrams with an Online Editor

Context

You are a scientist with extensive experience in representing and modeling scientific processes. The goal is to create a process diagram (BPMN 2.0) that depicts a typical scientific discovery process. The diagram should be compatible with Draw.io (or mxGraph) and meet the standards of scientific visualizations.

Instruction

Create a BPMN 2.0 diagram (schema documentation: https://www.omg.org/spec/BPMN/20100501/BPMN20.xsd) for Draw.io in XML format (based on the mxGraph documentation: https://jgraph.github.io/mxgraph/docs/js-api/files/index-txt.html), which depicts the following scientific process:

Start
1. Hypothesis (starting point; leads to 2)
2. Experiment (leads to 3)
3. Data Collection & Analysis / Evaluation of the Hypothesis (leads to 4a or 4b)
4a. Confirmation (leads to 1 and to 5)
4b. Refutation (leads to 1)
5. Repetition & Communication
End

Specifications

- Output the result as mxGraph-compatible XML code, embedded in a code box.
- Ensure a clear, tidy arrangement of elements in the diagram (e.g., top to bottom) so that the process flow is easy to follow.
- Use the standard BPMN 2.0 symbols (Start, End, Tasks, Gateways).
- Name all process steps precisely and clearly according to their function.

The context already explains that the diagram should be created in mxGraph format, which is supported by the online editor Draw.io. In addition, further background information can be integrated into the prompt, such as the target audience for the visualization (for example, for a term paper or a presentation to fellow students). Such information helps to better define the requirements for the design and level of detail of the diagram.

The instruction provides links to the official specifications and documentation of the formats used, BPMN 2.0 and mxGraph. This has the significant advantage that the language model is not solely dependent on stored model knowledge, but can refer to concrete guidelines and standards. In the case of BPMN, where several versions of the standard exist, the specification makes the instruction unambiguous. This significantly increases the likelihood of syntactically correct and content-precise output, while effectively reducing the risk of hallucinations in the generated markup code.

Furthermore, the instruction can be used to specify additional requirements, such as the desired level of detail (e.g., a simplified BPMN diagram) or specific requirements regarding layout and design (e.g., color coding), to further improve the readability and scientific expressiveness of the visualization.

Without the support of online tools, the SVG (Scalable Vector Graphics) image format is used. SVG—like HTML—is based on markup code, but it describes scalable vector graphics rather than web pages. SVG files enable high-resolution representations that can be scaled without loss, making them ideal for use in scientific papers. A particular advantage of SVG is that it can be imported into PowerPoint and, by ungrouping, converted into native shapes.

Another promising approach to creating visualizations is the use of specialized web libraries. Since the clear presentation of data also plays a central role on the web, a wide range of JavaScript libraries have been developed that can generate dynamic and interactive charts. Although these technologies were primarily designed for use on interactive websites, they are also suitable for integration into static documents, such as term or thesis papers. Table 8.1 provides an overview of selected JavaScript libraries for creating charts.

These libraries not only enable the display of classic chart types such as bar, pie, or scatter plots but also support more complex and less common forms of visualization, such as network diagrams, Sankey diagrams, or Mekko charts. Such representations offer significant added value for scientific analysis and presentation when dealing with complex data structures. Figure 8.3 illustrates various types of visualizations created using these web libraries.

To use JavaScript libraries for creating charts, they must be integrated and executed within an HTML document. The resulting visualizations can then be incorporated into scientific papers in various ways: charts can be captured via screenshots, or some libraries—such as Highcharts—offer integrated export functions that allow graphics to be saved directly in image format.

In their original use case, these libraries are primarily intended for generating interactive visualizations on the web. Users can dynamically filter data views, display details via tooltips, or actively explore different layers of the presentation. This interactivity cannot, by nature, be fully represented in static formats as required in term papers and theses. Nevertheless, interactive visualizations can help during the data analysis phase to grasp complex relationships more quickly and precisely.

Another advantage of using JavaScript-based charts is the ability to explicitly define specific formatting—such as fonts, color palettes, or size ratios—directly in the source code. This makes it easier to create a consistent visual style, which is

Table 8.1 JavaScript libraries for chart creation

Library	Chart Types (Selection)	Strengths
Plotly.js	Line, bar, scatter, 3D scatter/surface, heatmaps, maps, boxplots, violin, histogram	Designed for scientific plots and high-quality exports (SVG, PDF)
Vega-Lite	Line, bar, area, scatter, heatmap, maps, histogram, boxplot, layer/facets	Declarative grammar for reproducible graphics
Chart.js	Line, bar, pie/doughnut, radar, polar area, bubble, scatter, area	Quick creation of common chart types
Highcharts	Line, bar, pie, area, scatter, bubble, heatmap, treemap, gauge, polar, funnel, stock charts	Easy to get started, many export options (PNG, JPG, SVG, etc.)
ApexCharts	Line, bar, pie, area, scatter, heatmap, boxplot, bubble, treemap, radial bar	Attractive appearance with a wide range of types
ECharts (Apache)	Line, bar, maps, heatmaps, Sankey, sunburst, treemap, gauge, 3D variants	Can display complex and large datasets
D3.js	Any chart form via SVG, Canvas, or HTML	Extensive customization options
Cytoscape.js	Network/graph diagrams	Detailed visualization of networks

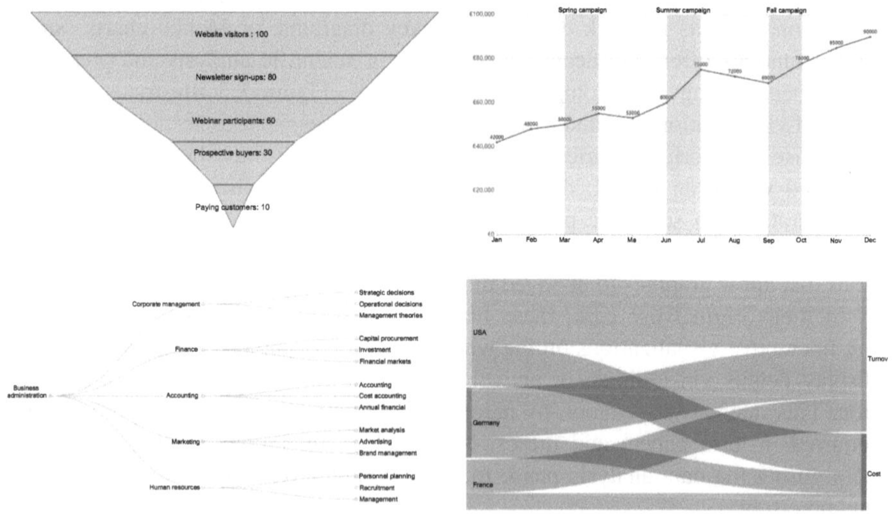

Fig. 8.3 Special chart types from JavaScript libraries

a significant relief compared to the often tedious manual formatting in traditional spreadsheet programs.

Prompt 8.6 provides an example of how a chart can be automatically created using a JavaScript library and prepared for integration into scientific papers.

Prompt 8.6: Creating Charts with a JavaScript Library

Context

You are a data visualization expert with experience in creating scientific charts. The goal is to create a heatmap for a seminar handout that clearly and professionally presents the use of different sales channels (online shop, store, telephone) by various age groups.

Instruction

Create a heatmap with vega.js (documentation: https://vega.github.io/vega-lite/docs/) that visualizes the following distribution of usage frequencies:

Schema: Customer group | Online shop, Store, Telephone
under 18 | 30, 15, 5
18-49 | 80, 50, 10
49-65 | 35, 40, 20
over 65 | 10, 25, 18

Specifications

- Display as a heatmap with layer text; numerical values should be centered in the cells (example: https://vega.github.io/vega-lite/examples/layer_text_heatmap.html)
- Aspect ratio 16:9
- Color scheme in the style of the New York Times (subtle, high-contrast, not overloaded color palette)
- Output format: HTML with integrated Vega.js JavaScript

In this prompt, the purpose is clearly defined: a chart is to be created that is suitable as a handout. The required data is either provided directly in the prompt or—in the case of larger datasets—alternatively attached as an Excel or CSV file (Comma-Separated Values). In this case, there is no need to specify the data explicitly in the prompt text. With regard to the graphic presentation, there are no strict requirements for layout or color scheme. Instead, a general style preference is formulated, namely an orientation toward the design of the New York Times. The language model interprets this requirement independently and implements it within its capabilities. The result of the prompt is an HTML file that can be opened and viewed directly in a web browser. Many AI chatbots also allow HTML to be previewed directly in the chat. For example, with Vega.js, a JSON (JavaScript Object Notation) can also be created and imported into the Vega-Lite

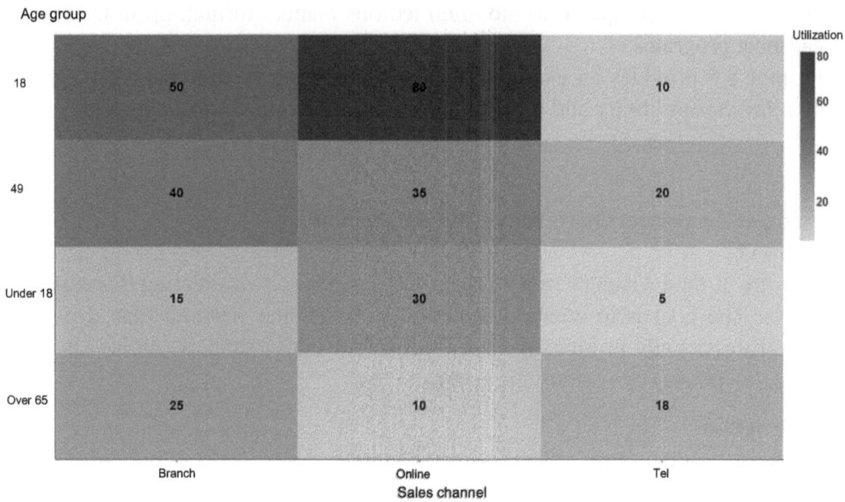

Fig. 8.4 Heatmap as the result of Prompt 8.6

online editor. This is comparable to the tools presented above, such as *Mermaid.live* or *RawGraphs.io*. The result of the prompt is shown in Fig. 8.4.

A key advantage of this approach lies in the flexibility to adapt data structures. The AI can easily be tasked with creating an alternative chart based on the existing data—for example, a pie chart to show the relative proportions of customer groups. Such operations can then be carried out automatically, without having to manually edit the dataset in a spreadsheet program. In the long term, it is advisable to acquire basic knowledge of the respective library syntax. This enables you to make minor adjustments independently and efficiently, without having to rely on the AI for every change, which can save time.

8.5 Do's and Don'ts

Do's

1. *Methodological responsibility*: Make the final decisions yourself and base them on recognized methodological literature; AI remains only an assistant.
2. *Prerequisite check*: Examine statistical assumptions or qualitative quality criteria before interpreting or reporting results.
3. *Source validation*: Always compare literature or key figures cited by the AI with reliable original sources to rule out hallucinations.
4. *Iterative dialogue*: Use follow-up questions to clarify ambiguities, adjust the level of detail, and systematically deepen understanding.
5. *Standards compliance*: Adhering to established procedures in your discipline helps increase acceptance among supervisors and reviewers.

6. *Clarity in visualization*: Create graphics that clearly, accessibly, and format-compliantly convey the core message; avoid overloaded effects.
7. *Data protection & ethics*: Check whether sensitive data has been anonymized before uploading to AI and whether the use of AI complies with your institution's guidelines.

Don'ts
1. *Black-box acceptance*: Do not simply refer to "the AI"; always explain how a result was obtained.
2. *Ignoring hallucinations*: Do not use sources, methods, or key figures that are not clearly verified.
3. *Automated full analysis*: Do not let the AI handle all statistics or interpretation without thinking or calculating for yourself.
4. *Unadjusted temperature*: Avoid creative settings (high temperature) for methodological fact prompts; they increase the risk of errors.
5. *Overly complex visualizations*: Do not use hard-to-read charts just because the AI suggests them.

References

Conde, J., Martínez, G., Reviriego, P., Gao, Z., Liu, S., & Lombardi, F. (2025). Can ChatGPT learn to count letters? *Computer, 58*(3), 96–99. https://doi.org/10.1109/MC.2024.3488313.

Karras, O., Lorenz, A.-L., & Auer, S. (2024). Präzisere Antworten: Sprachmodelle und Wissensgraphen für KI-gestützte Wissenschaft. *Forschung & Lehre*, (9/24), 672–674.

Kolasa, K., Goettsch, W., Petrova, G., & Berler, A. (2020). Without data, you're just another person with an opinion. *Expert Review of Pharmacoeconomics & Outcomes Research, 20*(2), 147–154. https://doi.org/10.1080/14737167.2020.1751612.

Lim, C. N.-H., Mra, A., Suliong, C., Rao, C. V., Aung, T., Sieman, J., Tin, W., Beshay, M. F. S., Payus, A. O., Lansing, M. G., Jeffree, M. S., Kadir, F. & Hayati, F. b. M. (2019). Recent advances in breast cancer diagnosis entering an era of precision medicine. *Borneo Journal of Medical Sciences (BJMS), 13*(1), 3–9. https://doi.org/10.51200/bjms.v13i1.1178.

Object Management Group. (2010). *Business Process Model and Notation (BPMN) 2.0* (No. 2.0).

Olmos-Vega, F. M., Stalmeijer, R. E., Varpio, L., & Kahlke, R. (2022). A practical guide to reflexivity in qualitative research: AMEE Guide No. 149. *Medical Teacher*, 1–11. https://doi.org/10.1080/0142159X.2022.2057287.

Perkins, M., & Roe, J. (2024). *Generative AI Tools in academic research: Applications and implications for qualitative and quantitative research methodologies*. https://arxiv.org/abs/2408.06872v1.

Ray, P. P. (2023). ChatGPT: A comprehensive review on background, applications, key challenges, bias, ethics, limitations and future scope. *Internet of Things and Cyber-Physical Systems, 3*, 121–154. https://doi.org/10.1016/j.iotcps.2023.04.003.

Schwarz, J. (2025). *Methodenberatung der Universität Zürich (UZH)*. https://www.methodenberatung.uzh.ch/.

Watson, S., Brezovec, E., & Romic, J. (2025). The role of generative AI in academic and scientific authorship: An autopoietic perspective. *AI & SOCIETY, 40*(5), 3225–3235. https://doi.org/10.1007/s00146-024-02174-w.

Final Touches: AI in Final Editing

9

Abstract

This chapter addresses the targeted use of artificial intelligence (AI) in final editing, the fine-tuning of academic papers. The chapter provides practical insights into how various AI applications contribute to quality improvement: they facilitate the detection and correction of formal errors, promote clear expression, and help develop coherent and comprehensible lines of argumentation. In addition, strategies for systematic literature critique and for checking the formal consistency of reference lists are explained. Furthermore, the role of AI in the final review and revision process is highlighted—with concrete prompts for different scenarios. Thus, the chapter offers a structured guide for the effective use of AI tools in the context of academic final editing, making their potential as well as their limitations transparent for students and instructors.

"There is no great writing, only great rewriting."
– Louis Brandeis (quoted in Guberman, 2015)

9.1 Software Support on the Home Stretch

The final phase of an academic paper is associated with particular pressure for many students. While content development often takes center stage, linguistic revision—the finishing touch—is frequently postponed. Shortly before submission, there is often little time left to optimize the text stylistically and formally. It is precisely in this phase that digital support tools can prove especially helpful.

Long before generative AI models, programs for spelling and grammar checking were already in use. Even though such tools vary in their capabilities, they

F. Lang, *Using Artificial Intelligence in Term Papers and Theses*,
https://doi.org/10.1007/978-3-662-73208-3_9

make a significant contribution to linguistic correctness and help ensure compliance with academic standards and the production of coherent scientific texts (Nurhayati, 2022).

With the advent of large language models, the capabilities of such tools have improved considerably. These systems not only detect formal errors such as spelling or punctuation mistakes with high precision, but also offer stylistic improvement suggestions. This allows academic texts to be linguistically refined and adapted to the required conventions. While error detection is not perfect—even LLMs occasionally overlook grammatical or orthographic errors (Wu et al., 2023)—the resulting quality gain is considerable in many cases.

In a study by Kim et al. (2025), in which students were required to write essays with AI support, the use of LLMs was consistently rated positively by the students for academic writing. In particular, the linguistic refinement was unanimously perceived as a clear advantage of AI. Added to this is the fact that AI tools are available at any time, and unlike human proofreading, no additional coordination effort is required.

As shown in Fig. 9.1, this chapter is divided into three thematic focal points. First, it explains how AI can support the linguistic revision of academic papers. This involves not only correcting formal aspects such as spelling, grammar, and punctuation, but also stylistic nuances that contribute to clearer, more precise expression. The second section addresses the literature base. Here, it is shown how AI can check both formal aspects—such as citation style and formatting—and content criteria such as the citability and relevance of the sources used. The chapter concludes with a section on argumentative revision. Using examples, it is illustrated how AI can help improve the coherence, consistency, and traceability of scientific arguments. A prompt for final proofreading rounds off the chapter and provides a practical guide for the last phase of text revision.

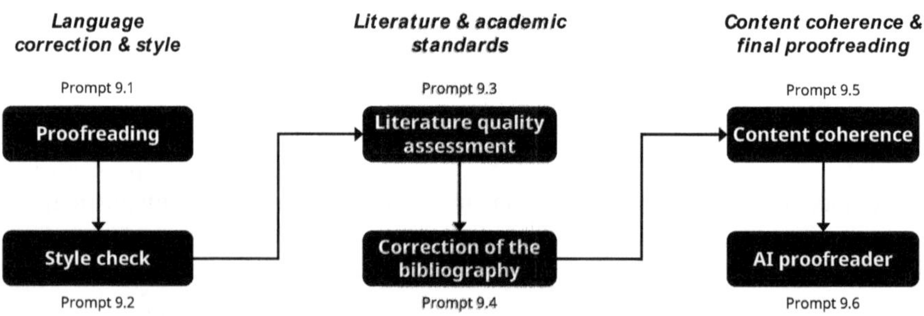

Fig. 9.1 AI for the final revision

9.2 Linguistic Correction & Style

At the latest by the end of an academic paper, careful linguistic revision is essential. To keep the effort manageable, it makes sense to regularly revise individual sections of text during the writing process. This allows linguistic weaknesses to be identified and corrected early on, rather than having to revise the entire manuscript under time pressure (Oehlrich, 2014).

In the context of so-called proofreading, spelling, grammar, and punctuation errors are primarily identified and corrected. This step not only provides linguistic refinement but also significantly contributes to the professional impression of the work. A formally flawless text signals care, competence, and respect for academic standards. Numerous digital tools are now available to support this step, many of which are based on artificial intelligence. Specialized applications such as Grammarly, LanguageTool, or even the proofreading mode in Microsoft Word already offer automated assistance at a high level. They reliably detect typical sources of error and suggest context-based improvements. General AI chatbots such as ChatGPT can also be used for linguistic revision. However, their quality is not always as consistent and specific as that of applications specifically designed for text correction.

With AI chatbots—due to output length limitations and better manageability with shorter inputs—the result is better if the entire paper is not checked at once, but rather section by section. Prompt 9.1 demonstrates how an LLM can check a specific section of a seminar or final paper for linguistic correctness. In this way, linguistic errors can be systematically identified and corrected without losing track or exceeding the performance limits of the AI system.

Prompt 9.1: Proofreading

Context

You are an experienced proofreader for academic texts. Your goal is to carefully check a text for linguistic correctness and consistency without unnecessarily changing the author's style. The focus is on formal aspects that could impair comprehensibility or linguistic quality.

Instruction

Please thoroughly check the following section of text and pay particular attention to the following:

1. Spelling errors—e.g., incorrect spellings such as "Ressources" instead of "Resources"
2. Punctuation errors—e.g., missing commas
3. Inconsistent spellings—e.g., alternating between "e-mail" and "email"
4. Grammatical inaccuracies—e.g., incorrect subject-verb agreement such as "The findings show"

5. Stylistic inconsistencies (only if they impair text comprehension)—e.g., awkward or ambiguous phrasing

Specifications

- Reproduce the complete original text.
- Mark all areas requiring correction with endnotes in square brackets (e.g., [1], [2], …).
- Afterwards, create a commented list of the endnotes, consisting of a brief description of the problem and a correction suggestion or a clear alternative formulation.
- Be sure to generally maintain the original writing style—changes should only be made if they are linguistically necessary or improve comprehension.

The prompt begins by clearly defining the assistant's role as a proofreader. The AI receives a task list focusing on typical sources of error (spelling, grammar, inconsistent spellings, and stylistic weaknesses), each illustrated with an example for the AI. Since AI chatbots do not offer direct text markup like word processors, a structured two-step approach is recommended. First, the complete original text is displayed to better locate the error in one's own work. The AI then lists numbered errors with explanations and suggestions for improvement. This makes it easy to review and revise the text.

Even though spelling check programs and AI-based tools reliably detect many errors, they do not fully replace human review. In particular, incomplete sentences, missing words, or stylistic inconsistencies are often overlooked by automated systems. A final review by a person is therefore essential to ensure linguistic correctness, content coherence, and good readability. Typically, friends or family are asked to conduct a "friends review" (Swoboda, 2023).

Classic spelling and grammar programs already do a good job of detecting formal errors. However, in academic writing, a precise, objective, and well-structured style is also important in addition to linguistic correctness. Academic writing means presenting complex content clearly and comprehensibly—without unnecessary jargon, linguistic digressions, or complicated sentence constructions. (Franck, 2024). Actual stylistic revision—such as simplifying complex sentence structures, avoiding redundant phrasing, or improving linguistic coherence—is made considerably easier by AI-supported tools, especially language models.

Language models can analyze text not only in its content context, but also imitate typical characteristics of certain roles and perspectives—such as that of a reviewer. This ability to adopt perspectives is particularly helpful for adapting the style of a paper to academic conventions.

An example of how a stylistic check can be initiated by an LLM is provided in Prompt 9.2. Here, too, revision should be done section by section, as input and output length limitations can cause relevant suggestions to be skipped if the text is too extensive. A detailed, systematic approach ensures high-quality stylistic optimization.

Prompt 9.2: Style Check

Context

You are an experienced academic writing coach specializing in academic style and language clarity in the field of [subject area]. Your support aims to revise a text so that it is stylistically polished, linguistically varied, and at the same time academically precise. Particular attention is paid to an appropriate and consistently maintained style that fits a seminar paper in the field of [subject area]. The target audience is professors who will evaluate the paper.

Instruction

Please analyze the following section of text with regard to its style, linguistic appropriateness, and readability. Pay particular attention to the following aspects:

1. Sentence length and readability: Are there sentences that are too long, convoluted, or difficult to understand?
2. Clarity and conciseness of expression: Are there overly abstract or unnecessarily complicated formulations that make the text less accessible?
3. Appropriateness of formal language for the target audience: Is the language technically correct and the tone appropriate for the academic context? Are unnecessary colloquialisms or stylistic inconsistencies avoided?

Specifications

- Provide concrete suggestions for improvement at the relevant points, e.g., through alternative formulations, shorter sentence structures, or more precise terms.
- The suggestions for improvement should strengthen the style of the seminar paper but not fundamentally change it.
- Show linguistic variation in the revision (synonyms, rewordings, transitions) without losing the content's impact or accuracy.
- Present the revision in comments on individual sentences.

The prompt not only defines the role of a writing coach but also specifies the relevant subject area. This takes into account the fact that different academic disciplines have specific requirements for style, structure, and expression. While the humanities typically involve more detailed argumentation and stylistic nuance, formal sciences such as mathematics are characterized by concise, precise, and highly accurate language.

At the same time, the prompt context makes it clear that academic papers are read and evaluated by professors. This note serves to clearly define the text's target audience and to align the linguistic standard accordingly. The stylistic revision by an LLM focuses in particular on three aspects: smooth readability, clear and formally appropriate expression, and target group appropriateness in language and structure.

The result is not a complete rewrite of the text, but a targeted optimization of the existing style. The AI generates concrete suggestions for improvement at the sentence and word level that respect the original text and maintain its structure. In this way, the individual expression is preserved but linguistically and stylistically elevated to the academic level of the respective discipline.

9.3 Literature & Academic Standards

Especially in student papers, where presenting the current state of research plays a central role, the selection, classification, and precise use of academic literature are of great importance. It is not enough to simply mention individual sources—rather, it should be clear which positions are represented in the academic community, how different theoretical approaches differ, and which perspectives are particularly relevant to the topic. Contrasting opinions or different disciplinary approaches should also be made visible.

AI can support this process by providing suggestions when certain viewpoints or important approaches are missing or underrepresented in the text. By analyzing the topic and content focus, it is possible to gain ideas on how to present the state of research more comprehensively and in a more balanced way. Such suggestions are especially helpful when one's own literature review needs to be critically examined and specifically supplemented. However, caution is advised: AI systems do not have full access to all academic publications, for example due to paywalls, and therefore cannot always fully or reliably reflect the current state of discussion. An exemplary prompt for such a literature critique is provided in Prompt 9.3.

Prompt 9.3: Literature Critique

Context

You are an experienced academic with extensive expertise in academic work and literature review. Your support aims to further develop a bibliography so that it is content-balanced, academically sound, and aligned with the current state of research—especially with regard to theses or publications.

Instruction

Please analyze the given bibliography based on the following three criteria:

1. Diversity: Does the bibliography cover different perspectives? For example, are various theoretical approaches represented?

2. Completeness: Are key viewpoints, schools of thought, or recent developments in the research field missing? Are there obvious gaps regarding the state of research?
3. Quality: Are the sources academically reliable literature (e.g., peer-reviewed journals, academic publishers, recognized authors)? Are there sources whose academic value is questionable?

Based on this, assess the quality of the bibliography and specify exactly where action is needed.

Specifications

- Provide a structured assessment for each of the three criteria mentioned (diversity, completeness, quality).
- Make concrete suggestions for improvement, such as adding current literature or relevant perspectives, reducing or replacing one-sided, outdated, or unreliable sources.
- The language should be objective, constructive, and student-friendly.

The prompt is intended to help specifically improve the handling of academic literature. The focus is not on simply expanding a bibliography, but on its critical reflection and systematic evaluation—a fundamental skill for anyone engaged in academic work. To this end, three central evaluation criteria are introduced: diversity, completeness, and quality. These make it possible to analyze the selection of literature in a structured way and to identify both content strengths and possible gaps. In addition, the prompt asks the AI to formulate concrete suggestions for improvement and to justify them in a comprehensible manner. The aim is not only to point out deficiencies, but to provide well-founded suggestions for targeted expansion and content sharpening of the literature base.

In addition to the content evaluation of a bibliography, its formal design is another often time-consuming task. Correct formatting requires a great deal of attention and detailed reworking—even when using reference management programs such as Citavi, Mendeley, or Zotero. These tools can automate most of the technical formatting, but they are not error-free, as bibliographic data are usually entered inconsistently or even incorrectly (Childress, 2011). For example, titles may be capitalized inconsistently—as in English-language publications, where some entries are formatted in title case throughout, while others use only an initial capital (sentence case). Another example is inconsistent spelling of author names, such as first names being sometimes written out and sometimes only given as initials. Information such as DOI (Digital Object Identifier) or page numbers within journal articles also often show inconsistencies, with some sources including them and others not. For this reason, a manual final check of the bibliography is indispensable. It is important to ensure consistency, completeness, and strict adherence to the required citation style. How artificial intelligence can provide targeted support here, for example by pointing out inconsistencies or detecting formatting errors, is demonstrated in Prompt 9.4.

Prompt 9.4: Bibliography Correction

Context

You are an experienced academic proofreader with in-depth knowledge of APA style (7th edition). Your task is to systematically check a bibliography for formal, consistent, and content accuracy so that it meets the requirements of an academic thesis. The basis for the assessment is the official APA reference standard (see https://apastyle.apa.org/instructional-aids/reference-examples.pdf).

Instruction

Please carefully check the given bibliography for the following three aspects:

1. Formal APA compliance: Is each source correctly formatted according to APA guidelines?
2. Consistency: Is the presentation of the literature consistent (e.g., are first names either always written out or always abbreviated)?
3. Completeness: Are details such as year of publication, editor, publisher, or DOI missing? Do in-text citations and bibliography entries match (every source in the text = in the bibliography and vice versa)?

Specifications

- List only the sources that require corrections.
- For each of these sources, provide both the original entry and the corrected suggestion.
- Indicate for each correction whether it is a formal error, a consistency error, or a content gap.

In this prompt, the AI is not only assigned a role and a subject context, but also a specific citation style, namely APA style. This citation style is regularly updated by the American Psychological Association (APA) and is one of the most widely used international standards. To ensure that the AI does not rely on outdated or mixed citation styles, it is also provided with an online PDF containing official reference examples. This ensures that the review is based on the most current version of the citation rules.

After clarifying this context, the AI checks the bibliography for formal, content, and consistency-related errors. Particularly helpful is the automated comparison between the bibliography and the in-text citations. In practice, copying and pasting from different documents can cause source links to be lost. What was originally an automatically linked source then appears only as unformatted text and is no longer updated by the reference management software. It is therefore advisable to make necessary corrections first in the reference management software so that the bibliographic data are corrected and can be reused in future work.

The final check of the bibliography should only take place at the very end of the writing process. This is because subsequent changes through automatic updating—such as when adding new sources—would otherwise overwrite previously made manual corrections. This final review is mainly intended to eliminate minor inconsistencies and typical formatting errors of reference management programs.

9.4 Content Coherence & Final Proofreading

As the deadline for submitting your work approaches, it is advisable to take a targeted look at the structure, comprehensibility, and clarity of your argumentation. Even a technically sound and methodologically rigorous paper can only be convincing if it is comprehensible. Scientific quality is demonstrated not only in the content, but also in how clearly and logically that content is conveyed.

For this purpose, Prompt 9.5 uses an AI-supported writing coach. This coach helps to check the text for logical coherence, a meaningful structure, and clear formulations. The AI coach also pays attention to whether certain assumptions remain unspoken in the text and should be made explicit. In this way, the AI coach helps sharpen the argumentation and make the work overall more understandable and convincing, without changing your personal style.

Prompt 9.5: Content Coherence

Context

You are an experienced writing coach specializing in academic writing and argumentative clarity. Your goal is to help me analyze and specifically improve a section of text.

Instruction

Please critically analyze the following section of text with regard to its argumentative and structural quality. Pay particular attention to three aspects:

1. Argumentative coherence: Assess whether the argumentation is logically structured. Identify possible breaks or logical leaps in the line of reasoning.
2. Structure and clarity: Suggest ways to improve the organization and presentation of the text to make the line of reasoning clearer for readers.
3. Implicit assumptions: Examine whether the text is based on unstated premises or background assumptions. Identify these and explain whether and how they should be made explicit.

Specifications

- Present your analysis in a structured way—for example, as bullet points or short paragraphs, organized according to the three areas of analysis.
- Additionally, create a revision-oriented to-do list, dividing the tasks into the categories Must, Should, and Can.
- Use objective, constructive language aimed at improvement, not mere criticism.
- Avoid sweeping judgments—substantiate all comments concretely with reference to the text.

As an alternative to the writing coach, you can also adopt the perspective of an evaluating professor with a particularly scrutinizing, critical reading style. This perspective can help to specifically recognize typical expectations for academic work and to uncover possible weaknesses that could negatively affect the assessment. The writing coach, on the other hand, has the advantage of acting in a more supportive manner and thus focusing not only on criticism but also on constructive suggestions.

To receive differentiated and targeted suggestions for improvement, it is advisable to divide the work into individual sections and have them checked by the AI step by step. In this way, content coherence can be reflected on and specifically improved chapter by chapter, without important feedback being lost due to an overly extensive input.

It should be noted that the AI only provides supportive suggestions. The responsibility for selecting and implementing these suggestions remains with the author. Careful consideration must be given to which recommendations actually contribute to improving your own work, how well they fit into the overall content and argumentative context, and whether they usefully complement your individual writing style and the subject-specific requirements.

At the end of the writing process, the work is often given to a friend or family member for proofreading or review. By using AI tools in a targeted way, most language errors—such as spelling, grammar, or punctuation—can already be identified and corrected in advance. As a result, traditional proofreading is becoming less important, since formal errors rarely affect the overall impression of the work. At this stage, the greater value lies in reviewing for comprehensibility, logical consistency of the argumentation, and the overall impression of the work.

Final editing can also be usefully prepared with the help of AI before the work is handed over to a third person for review. The AI performs an initial comprehensive review, which not only makes the subsequent manual check easier, but can also significantly improve the linguistic and structural quality of the final version in advance.

In practice, it is also often the case that buffer times are tight and there is no longer an opportunity to have the work reviewed externally at the end of the writing process. In such cases, the AI can take on the role of a final proofreader and help identify remaining ambiguities, stylistic weaknesses, or structural breaks. An example of how a suitable prompt for such a final proofreading can be designed is shown in Prompt 9.6.

Prompt 9.6: AI Proofreader

Context

You are an experienced editor who reviews academic papers with a clear, critical eye. You provide your feedback directly, honestly, and without sugarcoating—with the goal of promoting quality. Your assessment is not diplomatic, but professionally sharp and precise.

Instruction

Critically and unreservedly evaluate the present academic work using the following guiding questions. The aim is to provide honest, tough, but constructive feedback that helps students make substantial improvements.

1. Content quality: Is the research question clearly formulated and consistently addressed? Are the arguments logically structured and easy to follow—or does the text jump around? Is the literature integrated meaningfully, critically, and on a sound basis—or merely cited? Is there evidence of original work—for example, through reflection, evaluation, or independent conclusions?
2. Structure & organization: Is the outline logical and appropriate for the subject? Are the chapters clearly separated, functionally designed, and complete? Does the introduction precisely introduce the topic—or does it remain vague? Does the conclusion clearly summarize the main findings or merely repeat previous content? Are there meaningful transitions, or is the text a patchwork?
3. Scientific working methods & critical reflection: Is there a clear distinction between personal opinion and scientific knowledge? Are quotations properly referenced, sources transparently indicated? Is the methodological approach comprehensible and correct? Does the work go beyond mere reporting—or does it remain at the level of a summary?

Specifications

- Respond directly, critically, and without softening—no sugarcoating.
- Use clear, concise language. Make it clear where the problems are—and why.
- Identify specific weaknesses and, if necessary, give tough judgments ("not sufficient," "too vague," "no argumentation evident").
- If appropriate, provide brief suggestions for improvement, but without a pedagogical tone—the task is assessment, not guidance.

This prompt is a deliberately sharply formulated correction tool, designed as a counterbalance to milder revision approaches (such as the AI writing coach from Prompt 9.5 or stylistically oriented fine-tuning prompts). The academic work is viewed here from the perspective of a very critical subject editor. The aim is not to provide motivational or diplomatic feedback, but to clearly, directly, and unvarnishedly identify substantial weaknesses. The AI takes on a professional, detached role and applies strict standards of scientific quality.

In this way, students can specifically identify weaknesses and further develop their work before submission along three central dimensions—content quality, structure and organization, and scientific working methods and reflection. The prompt thus simulates realistic assessment situations in which tough judgments can also be made. This rigor is not a disadvantage, but a specific advantage of AI: While feedback from personal contacts is often softened out of consideration and sometimes received defensively by authors, the social context is absent with AI. This makes it easier to accept criticism objectively and reflect on it critically.

At the same time, using the prompt requires exactly this active role from students: The ability to distinguish relevant and helpful feedback from less appropriate comments and to implement it constructively is crucial for further developing your own work. Those who master this process not only improve the quality of their own text, but also strengthen their own scientific judgment.

9.5 Do's and Don'ts

Do's

1. *Iterative section editing*: Break long papers into manageable sections and go through them step by step with AI prompts (correction, style, argumentation); inputs that are too long can overload the model.
2. *Specialized tools over general-purpose LLMs*: Use correction programs for spelling/grammar, reference management software for citations; use AI chatbots as a supplement.
3. *Consistency check for references*: Use AI to specifically search for missing information, mixed citation styles, or duplicates, and then manually correct them in the reference management program.
4. *Provide supplementary documents*: Link or upload documents such as the official citation standard and let the AI "learn" from them.
5. *Argumentative coherence check*: Use AI as a writing coach to uncover logical breaks, implicit assumptions, and weak transitions.
6. *Preserve style*: Formulate prompt instructions so that your individual tone is maintained and only necessary changes are made.

Don'ts

1. *Last-minute changes without follow-up check*: Any late text change can throw off cross-references, figure lists, or references.
2. *Stylistic smoothing to the point of unrecognizability*: Overly aggressive rewrites can dilute your own voice and argumentative sharpness.
3. *Focusing only on grammar*: Spelling may be correct, but content precision, terminology, or subject context are not necessarily ensured.

References

Childress, D. (2011). Citation tools in academic libraries. *Reference & User Services Quarterly, 51*(2), 143–152. https://doi.org/10.5860/rusq.51n2.143.

Franck, N. (2024). *Schreiben im Studium: Wie Hausarbeiten und andere Texte gelingen. Kompakte Antworten auf die 22 wichtigsten Fragen*. Springer VS. https://doi.org/10.1007/978-3-658-45377-0.

Guberman, R. (2015). *Point taken: How to write like the world's best judges*. Oxford University Press.

Kim, J., Yu, S., Detrick, R., & Li, N. (2025). Exploring students' perspectives on Generative AI-assisted academic writing. *Education and Information Technologies, 30*(1), 1265–1300. https://doi.org/10.1007/s10639-024-12878-7.

Nurhayati, D. A. W. (2022). The relevance of adopting proofreading tools to maintain academic writing integrity and coherence text. *Indonesian Journal of EFL and Linguistics, 7*(2), 373. https://doi.org/10.21462/ijefl.v7i2.547.

Oehlrich, M. (2014). *Wissenschaftliches Arbeiten und Schreiben: Schritt für Schritt zur Bachelor- und Master-Thesis in den Wirtschaftswissenschaften*. Springer. https://doi.org/10.1007/978-3-662-44099-5.

Swoboda, M. (2023). *Wissenschaftlich schreiben leicht gemacht: Ein Leitfaden für Architektur- und Designstudiengänge*. Springer Vieweg. https://doi.org/10.1007/978-3-658-42166-3.

Wu, H., Wang, W., Wan, Y., Jiao, W., & Lyu, M. (2023). *ChatGPT or grammarly? Evaluating ChatGPT on grammatical error correction benchmark*. https://arxiv.org/abs/2303.13648v1.

Conclusion: Final Outlook and Concluding Remarks

10

Abstract

This chapter analyzes the role of artificial intelligence (AI) in academic work and situates it within the historical development of digital technologies. It describes how AI, and in particular large language models, are increasingly taking on tasks in research and teaching, such as text analysis, structuring literature, or selecting methods. These systems enable the automation of repetitive work steps and create space for conceptual thinking. At the same time, the chapter identifies key challenges, such as lack of transparency, potential biases, and the risk of homogenizing scientific forms of expression. It emphasizes the importance of scientific integrity, methodological diligence, and critical reflection when dealing with AI-supported tools. Responsibility for scientific content remains entirely with the researchers. The chapter also outlines future application scenarios and derives new competency requirements, as the confident use of AI is becoming a key qualification in the academic context.

"A computer can never be held accountable, therefore a computer must never make a management decision."
– From an IBM training manual from 1979 (quoted in Bonderud, 2025).

10.1 Positioning of AI

Artificial intelligence, especially in the form of large language models, marks a profound transformation in academic work. Contrary to widespread fears, this transformation does not necessarily entail a loss of academic standards or an erosion of academic integrity. Rather, technological progress opens up new opportunities: for greater efficiency, better access to knowledge, and more individualized support for the development of academic skills.

F. Lang, *Using Artificial Intelligence in Term Papers and Theses*,
https://doi.org/10.1007/978-3-662-73208-3_10

A look back at past developments makes it clear that technological innovations have always shaped and changed university studies. As recently as the 1990s, studying was closely tied to physical presence in libraries. Computers, if available at all, were stationary devices for students. Internet access was limited and rare outside universities. Academic work therefore meant working through shelves and archive rooms, borrowing journal volumes, and queuing at photocopiers to duplicate relevant passages. The digitization of library collections and the widespread expansion of internet access fundamentally changed these conditions. Texts became searchable, library catalogs were digitized, and articles became available via remote access. Libraries thus evolved from mere storage facilities into multifunctional learning and service centers (Arms, 2012; Suri, 2013).

These changes were accompanied by the introduction of digital tools to support academic work. Reference management programs, for example, have since enabled users to systematically record sources, organize them thematically, format citations correctly, or create excerpts. Today, these applications are considered a self-evident part of academic work and have established themselves as helpful additions.

Despite these far-reaching advances, which the overwhelming majority of students and instructors would not want to do without, critical voices have never been completely silenced. Especially in the course of the digitalization of academic work, there have been repeated warnings that easier access to knowledge could be accompanied by a decline in depth. Critics have lamented increasing superficiality in dealing with texts, declining reading comprehension, and reduced reading depth (see, e.g., Degele, 1999; Carr, 2010; Dakakni & Safa, 2023).

Artificial intelligence marks the next major revolution in academic work, and the changes it brings are likely to be even more far-reaching. Even today, AI is used in numerous phases of the research process—whether in studies or in science—often in ways exemplified in this book: language models are used to revise text drafts, identify and structure relevant literature, or generate suggestions for suitable research questions, methodological designs, and argumentative structures. The potential is particularly evident where AI can take over repetitive, time-consuming tasks. These include extracting structured information from large, unstructured text collections, automated classification of data, or the formal standardization of citation styles and text layouts (Burger et al., 2023; Grimaldi & Ehrler, 2023).

Artificial intelligence makes it possible to automate small-scale, time-intensive tasks and thus focus on the core conceptual and substantive tasks. By using appropriate systems, activities can be carried out more consistently and with a lower risk of error. In addition, AI can help to introduce objectivity and additional quality assurance into academic work. In the linguistic formulation of academic texts, even authors who do not consider themselves particularly eloquent can use AI-based writing assistance to formulate their texts clearly, in a structured manner, and with stylistic appeal (Grimaldi & Ehrler, 2023; van Noorden & Perkel, 2023).

Despite the many potentials of using AI in academic work, critical voices are also increasing, pointing to fundamental challenges and risks. A central criticism concerns the lack of transparency in many AI systems. The exact functioning of large language models, their training data, and algorithmic decision-making processes are often not openly accessible or comprehensible. This makes it difficult to reproduce results—a central quality criterion of scientific research (Ball, 2023). In a scientific culture based on traceability and verifiability, this lack of transparency represents a structural problem.

Moreover, AI systems carry the risk not only of adopting existing biases but even amplifying them through systematic application. Prejudices embedded in training data can creep unnoticed into academic texts, analyses, or argument structures, thus contributing to the reproduction of social imbalances. The use of AI tools can also lead to increasing homogenization of academic texts. Individual writing styles, discipline-specific forms of expression, and culturally shaped communication styles recede into the background (Grimaldi & Ehrler, 2023). This contradicts the principle of pluralism in science. Last but not least, there are concerns that key academic skills—such as systematically formulating research questions, methodological approaches, or critical text analysis—could fall by the wayside due to the use of AI. If students and researchers rely too heavily on automated suggestions and evaluations, there is a risk of losing methodological independence and judgment (Burger et al., 2023). This problem is exacerbated by the fact that many users still lack a solid education in dealing with AI-based methods (van Noorden & Perkel, 2023).

In the field of scientific publishing, so-called paper mills—institutions that produce articles en masse—are a problem. AI makes it possible to generate large numbers of seemingly plausible but substantively worthless articles. Similarly, AI also makes it easier for students to create plagiarized and fake academic texts. While such practices are a clear violation of academic integrity, there were already ways to deliberately deceive before. However, the low threshold created by AI significantly lowers the barriers to dishonest behavior. Precisely because it is now effortless to generate texts that appear academic, there remains skepticism among many about the use of these new technologies (Grimaldi & Ehrler, 2023; van Noorden & Perkel, 2023).

Looking to the future, it can be assumed that AI will not only be an established but an integral part of academic work. Already today, the vast majority of researchers expect that AI will play a central, if not essential, role in their disciplines in the coming years (van Noorden & Perkel, 2023). It is to be expected that the current applications of AI are not the end but rather the starting point for further developments. In particular, large language models open up new perspectives for data collection. For example, AI can be used to simulate human participants in surveys, interviews, or behavioral experiments. These virtual subjects make it possible to test initial hypotheses, vary samples, or try out methodological designs in advance, without the organizational effort of real recruitment. This can be especially helpful in the methodological training of students to teach empirical techniques. Furthermore, this approach makes it possible to test interventions first in risk-free AI simulations before applying them to real people—a factor that is especially relevant for sensitive research questions (Grossmann et al., 2023).

New potentials are also emerging in the area of quality assurance. In the future, AI can help to detect academic irregularities such as plagiarism, fabricated results, or methodological flaws at an early stage, thereby improving the reliability of academic work (Gibney, 2025). It is also conceivable that AI will systematically support the assessment process of academic work in the future and automatically detect sources of error and methodological weaknesses (Thelwall, 2025). Students could thus use automated pre-checks to receive feedback on substantive weaknesses or formal errors. Nevertheless, the assessment of academic performance remains a genuinely human task. This is not only a matter of ethical responsibility but also a necessity in view of those abilities that no machine currently possesses: the ability for nuanced judgment, evaluative contextualization, and critical thinking. Only humans can grasp all these dimensions in their entirety and evaluate them responsibly (Ebadi et al., 2025).

The core values of science remain unchanged and essential even in an AI-supported research landscape. However, the way we conduct research is being profoundly transformed by AI. The challenge is to harness the potential of AI without compromising academic quality. Or, as Grimaldi and Ehrler (2023, p. 879) succinctly put it in their closing sentence: "Like our forest-dwelling ancestors that discovered fire, we need to be mindful of the unwanted consequences of our exciting advances, to reap their benefits without setting our homes ablaze."

10.2 Conclusion for the Use of AI

In conclusion, it can be stated that artificial intelligence in the form of large language models—despite their impressive capabilities—still counts as weak AI. Such systems generate texts based on statistical probabilities, without possessing their own consciousness, intention, or substantive understanding. They imitate language, but they do not understand what they write. Accordingly, responsibility for substantive accuracy, argumentative coherence, and academic integrity remains entirely with the authors of academic work. AI can support the work, but it can never replace what is at the core of academic work: an independent process of discovery, driven by critical reflection, methodological rigor, and academic responsibility.

To productively integrate AI into the academic work process, a fundamental understanding of its functioning and limitations is required—as explained in detail in Chap. 2. Only those who understand the principles of statistical modeling and the technical limitations can properly interpret the resulting outputs. The ability to critically evaluate AI-generated content thus becomes a new form of academic competence.

A central prerequisite for the use of AI in the academic context remains the preservation of academic integrity. This includes taking ultimate responsibility for the results, critically monitoring AI-supported processes, and providing subject-matter oversight. Academic work must not become a purely technical operation, but must always be based on substantive judgment, methodological care, and ethical reflection. AI may provide suggestions, but it is always the human who decides on their relevance, accuracy, and appropriateness.

Another fundamental principle concerns transparency. The use of AI must be documented and disclosed—not out of mistrust toward the authors, but as a matter of the traceability of academic methods. Anyone who uses technical aids in the academic process must indicate this—analogous to the disclosure of other forms of support and sources. Only in this way does academic work remain verifiable and reproducible.

Responsible use of AI is also bound by ethical, legal, and social standards. Its use must not lead to the systematic disadvantage of particular groups, nor to the loss of diversity, creativity, or pluralism in academic discourse. Ultimately, technological progress must not come at the expense of those values that define science as an open, socially responsible practice.

Throughout this book, a wide range of applications for artificial intelligence in academic writing and thinking have been presented, from topic selection and structuring to literature research, data analysis, and method selection, all the way to linguistic refinement.

As has been shown, AI can provide valuable support throughout the entire academic work process—under the conditions outlined above. Yet academic thinking, judgment, and writing remain human tasks. It is therefore essential that students acquire the necessary skills for dealing with AI—not only for academic success, but also as preparation for a working world in which the competent use of AI will become a key qualification.

10.3 Closing Remarks

As the numerous examples in this book make clear, AI is already changing the way academic work is done—both in university studies and in academic research. This change does not come without consequences, as it shifts the requirements for academic competence. Whereas in the past, aspects such as linguistic correctness, stylistic expressiveness, and formal accuracy were relevant assessment criteria, today, substantive clarity, conceptual coherence, and methodological independence are coming to the fore. What once stood out positively, such as flawless spelling or clean punctuation, is now taken for granted thanks to AI support.

The change affects not only the form but also the substantive depth of academic work. In literature work, for example, AI has made it fundamentally easier to identify sources and to generate summaries automatically. Precisely for this reason, the demands on the depth of analysis are also increasing. No longer is it enough to simply reproduce content; what is required is its structured, critical synthesis. Students must not only process literature, but also place it in an argumentative context, identify research gaps, and take a reasoned position.

This pattern is not new: similar developments could already be observed with the digitization of literature or the introduction of calculators or statistical software. The tools became more powerful, and with them, expectations for academic results increased. AI, too, does not lower academic standards, but rather advances them, as technical facilitation is accompanied by increased demands for substantive depth and methodological rigor.

These higher standards have not yet been implemented everywhere—not least because instructors themselves often still need to familiarize themselves with the new technologies in practice. However, in the medium term, academic training will be noticeably transformed, moving toward a higher level of expectation that not only utilizes technological possibilities but also builds upon them.

The quality of academic performance will increasingly be measured by how competently technological support is integrated into the process of discovery—without losing sight of responsibility for content, method, and ethics. AI is therefore not a substitute for academic thinking, but a tool to elevate it to a new level. What matters is that AI is used wisely, transparently, and responsibly. For it is not the technology that determines academic quality, but the human being who knows how to use it.

References

Arms, W. Y. (2012). The 1990s: The formative years of digital libraries. *Library Hi Tech, 30*(4), 579–591. https://doi.org/10.1108/07378831211285068.

Ball, P. (2023). Is AI leading to a reproducibility crisis in science? *Nature, 624*(7990), 22–25. https://doi.org/10.1038/d41586-023-03817-6.

Bonderud, D. (2025, June 20). *AI decision-making: Where do businesses draw the line?* IBM. https://www.ibm.com/think/insights/ai-decision-making-where-do-businesses-draw-the-line.

Burger, B., Kanbach, D. K., Kraus, S., Breier, M., & Corvello, V. (2023). On the use of AI-based tools like ChatGPT to support management research. *European Journal of Innovation Management, 26*(7), 233–241. https://doi.org/10.1108/EJIM-02-2023-0156.

Carr, N. G. (2010). *The shallows: What the internet is doing to our brains* (1. ed.). Norton.

Dakakni, D., & Safa, N. (2023). Reading patterns, scanning, and the "Control F"/search icon: How students really (don't) read. *International Research in Education, 11*(1), 128. https://doi.org/10.5296/ire.v11i1.20943.

Degele, N. (1999). „Doing Knowledge“: Vom gebildeten zum informierten Wissen. In C. Honegger, S. Hradil, & F. Traxler (Eds.), *Grenzenlose Gesellschaft?* (pp. 459–470). VS Verlag. https://doi.org/10.1007/978-3-322-93332-4_41.

Ebadi, S., Nejadghanbar, H., Salman, A. R., & Khosravi, H. (2025). Exploring the impact of generative AI on peer review: Insights from journal reviewers. *Journal of Academic Ethics.* Online first. https://doi.org/10.1007/s10805-025-09604-4.

Gibney, E. (2025). AI tools are spotting errors in research papers: Inside a growing movement. *Nature*. Online first. https://doi.org/10.1038/d41586-025-00648-5.

Grimaldi, G., & Ehrler, B. (2023). AI et al.: Machines are about to change scientific publishing forever. *ACS Energy Letters, 8*(1), 878–880. https://doi.org/10.1021/acsenergylett.2c02828.

Grossmann, I., Feinberg, M., Parker, D. C., Christakis, N. A., Tetlock, P. E., & Cunningham, W. A. (2023). AI and the transformation of social science research. *Science (New York, N.Y.), 380*(6650), 1108–1109. https://doi.org/10.1126/science.adi1778.

Suri, R. E. (2013). Bibliotheken im digitalen Zeitalter: Digitalisierung bietet neue Chancen und Herausforderungen. *Bulletin SEV/VSE*, Vol. 104. https://doi.org/10.3929/ETHZ-A-009935854.

Thelwall, M. (2025). Evaluating research quality with Large Language Models: An analysis of ChatGPT's effectiveness with different settings and inputs. *Journal of Data and Information Science, 10*(1), 7–25. https://doi.org/10.2478/jdis-2025-0011.

van Noorden, R., & Perkel, J. M. (2023). AI and science: What 1,600 researchers think. *Nature, 621*(7980), 672–675. https://doi.org/10.1038/d41586-023-02980-0.

MIX
Papier aus verantwortungsvollen Quellen
Paper from responsible sources
FSC® C105338

If you have any concerns about our products,
you can contact us on
ProductSafety@springernature.com

In case Publisher is established outside the EU,
the EU authorized representative is:
Springer Nature Customer Service Center GmbH
Europaplatz 3, 69115 Heidelberg, Germany

Printed by Libri Plureos GmbH
in Hamburg, Germany